Daughters of (Re)Imagined Early Childhood Education

Contemporary Perspectives on the Lives of Teachers

Series Editors
Carol R. Rinke and Lynnette Mawhinney

Contemporary Perspectives on the Lives of Teachers provides a forum for innovative research related to the lives of teachers around the world. This series seeks to highlight the voices of teachers themselves in constructing their own lives and careers and welcomes multiple methodologies and theoretical perspectives for doing so. It also seeks pioneering research that identifies, analyzes, and addresses current challenges facing teachers in today's classrooms nationally and internationally. The series strives to serve as an indispensable voice for the personal and the professional in teaching, synthesizing research that works toward an effective and committed teaching force for today's schools, students, and the teachers themselves.

OTHER TITLES IN THE SERIES

Mentoring as Critically Engaged Praxis (2020)
Deirdre Cobb-Roberts and Talia Esnard

Opportunities and Challenges in Teacher Recruitment and Retention (2019)
Carol R. Rinke and Lynnette Mawhinney

Daughters of (Re)Imagined Early Childhood Education

Reflective Narratives of Black Women Educators in Texas During COVID-19

Edited by

Meghan L. Green

Erikson Institute, USA

United Kingdom – North America – Japan
India – Malaysia – China

Emerald Publishing Limited
Emerald Publishing, Floor 5, Northspring, 21-23 Wellington Street, Leeds LS1 4DL

First edition 2026

Copyright © Emerald Publishing Limited 2026.
All rights of reproduction in any form reserved.

Cover photo: Atlas studio/iStock

Reprints and permissions service
Contact: www.copyright.com

No part of this book may be reproduced, stored in a retrieval system, transmitted in any form or by any means electronic, mechanical, photocopying, recording or otherwise without either the prior written permission of the publisher or a licence permitting restricted copying issued in the UK by The Copyright Licensing Agency and in the USA by The Copyright Clearance Center. Any opinions expressed in the chapters are those of the authors. Whilst Emerald makes every effort to ensure the quality and accuracy of its content, Emerald makes no representation implied or otherwise, as to the chapters' suitability and application and disclaims any warranties, express or implied, to their use.

British Library Cataloguing in Publication Data
A catalogue record for this book is available from the British Library

ISBN: 978-1-80592-113-4 (Print hardback)
ISBN: 978-1-80592-115-8 (Print paperback)
ISBN: 978-1-80592-112-7 (Ebook)
ISBN: 978-1-80592-114-1 (Epub)

Typeset by TNQ Tech
Cover design by TNQ Tech

CONTENTS

About the Editor vii

About the Contributors ix

Preface xi

1 Letting Go to Grow 1
 Bobbi Reagor Marshall

2 Shifting and Blooming 9
 Myah Breaux

3 Destiny Detours 19
 Krystle Dior Armstrong

4 Unsolicited Favour 29
 Alexis E. Moore

5 Question Everything, Always Speak Up 41
 Carson B. Willis

6 A New Respect 49
 Deidra Parker

7 Rock Steady: An Autoethnography Exploring My Lived
 Experiences During Dual Pandemics 59
 Meghan L. Green

Closing 73
 Meghan L. Green

ABOUT THE EDITOR

Meghan L. Green EdD is an Assistant Professor at Erikson Institute in Chicago, IL. As an arts-based qualitative researcher, she uses multiple modes of creative representation to reflect on her positionality and to craft her story as a cis Black queer woman engaging in critically informed research methodologies within this time and space. Her scholarship centres Black feminist thought and endarkened feminist epistemology within early childhood settings, specifically highlighting the diverse lived experiences of Black early childhood educators through arts-based qualitative inquiry methods including, but not limited to, autoethnography, endarkened narrative inquiry, Photovoice, and poetic inquiry.

ABOUT THE CONTRIBUTORS

Krystle Dior Armstrong is a Special Education Co-Teacher, YMCA Group Leader, and full-time online student at Grand Canyon University, pursuing a Bachelor of Science in Behavioral Health. She is deeply passionate about advocating for individuals who are often overlooked, misunderstood, or living with disabilities and mental health challenges. After graduation, Krystle plans to step beyond the traditional classroom setting to develop accessible, personalized educational materials and behavioral resources. Her mission is to empower and uplift marginalized populations – meeting them where they are and helping them reach their fullest potential.

Myah Breaux is a former English Language Arts teacher who taught at the primary level in the Dallas/Fort Worth Metroplex of Texas, where she also served as the English Language Arts Vertical Content Lead on her campus. Her experience in the classroom deepened her commitment to ensuring that all students have access to equitable, high-quality education. As a former educator, she firmly believes that literacy is a foundational tool for empowerment and opportunity: if you can read, you can do anything. She now works in the nonprofit sector, continuing to advocate for educational equity by supporting schools and communities through meaningful programs and partnerships.

Alexis E. Moore, MEd in Educational Leadership from Grand Canyon University, specializing in administration and student support services, serves as a secondary educator, specializing in literacy intervention, journalism/creative writing through Title I public schools in Fort Worth, TX. Her work centres on educating and leading Black and Brown students from various backgrounds towards college and career readiness to ultimately succeed despite the challenges. Alexis enjoys the outdoors, volunteering in her community, and being a mother to her loving daughter.

Deidra Parker is a primary teacher with a Master of Art in Teaching. She also graduated with honours when she received her Bachelor of Science in

Human Services focussing on Family Child Services. Deidra has been teaching primary scholars for seven years. She received teacher of the year her first year of teaching and has been lead grade level chair for five years. She is also a recognized designated teacher with the Texas Education Agency, which means she exhibits above-average teaching practices that positively impact student academic growth. Deidra believes children should experience a lifetime of growth, protection, and experiences that will enhance the entirety of adulthood.

Bobbi Reagor Marshall, MA, is an early education teacher and graduate student at the University of Arizona Global Campus. She received her Master's degree in Early Educational Leadership in March of 2023 and continues her journey in building educational awareness in urban communities. Her vision is to allow families from all financial hardships to be able to place their children in early educational facilities that provide parent education, respect a child's creativity, cognitive, and social-emotional growth and builds a community that offers diverse learning.

Carson B. Willis is currently a doctoral student studying Clinical Psychology. She previously taught fourth-grade English Language Arts at Uplift Ascend Primary in Fort Worth, TX for three years. She graduated from the University of Oklahoma and is a Teach for America alumni.

PREFACE

Stories matter. Perspectives matter. Critical race theorists leverage the multiple vantage points of historically marginalized people to find the balance in our everyday experiences (Delgado & Stefancic, 2001). My views on my maternal grandmother, whose formal schooling ended in the sixth grade, have been significantly shaped by my Black feminist worldview. She was a poor Black woman in south Louisiana in the 1940s who meticulously observed those around her and then used that knowledge to provide for her family. Her daily experiences helped her solve practical problems. She extended that compassion to those in her community who may have needed assistance as well. The practical life lessons she taught me often complement the academic knowledge I received in my doctoral classes.

As a researcher and early childhood teacher educator, I utilize Black feminist thought to extend this intergenerational bridge and to create a space intended to attest to how the lives of Black women like my grandmother are situated in the larger context of race, gender, sexual orientation, and class. *Daughters of (Re)Imagined Early Childhood Education: Reflective Narratives of Black Women Educators in Texas During COVID-19* provides a look into the narratives of Black women in north Texas who brought themselves fully into early learning settings from 2020 to 2022. It is important to ground the present work in the historical context of social activism in response to systemic anti-Black police violence.

Historical Context of Police Brutality and Social Activism in the United States

Aiello (2023) noted that the history of police brutality in the United States (US) began with slave patrols as 'white authorities used violence against Black lives and bodies as a form of containment for slave labour' (p. 3). Scholars have long considered the connection between local forms of political activism in Black communities and race-based police brutality in the southern sector of the US (Aiello, 2023). Oftentimes, carceral aggression preceded Black residents' actions against longstanding mistreatment. As Black folks' calls for justice and equitable treatment amplified over the decades, police brutality in urban and rural areas across the south only increased. By the passage of the Voting Rights Act of 1965, it had become a common form of intimidation that was cemented into the fabric of law enforcement in the nation. Racialized policing (Aiello, 2023) impacted communities of Colour across the country during the height of social movements in the mid-to late-20th century. Institutionalized violence against Black communities in the US has consistently spurred protest movements advocating for the abolition of the carceral state (Carruthers, 2018). The narratives presented in this book align with the collective imagination Carruthers (2018) referenced as they are a part of our legacy of struggle as Black women and embody our commitment to liberation through service.

Amidst the uncertainty of a global pandemic and the audacious eruption of anti-Black racial violence in the US in 2020, my co-authors and I found strength in our bonds as educators on the same campus. These shared bonds – built initially on shared identity markers such as race and gender – developed over time due to our collective lived experiences during one of the most traumatic periods of our lives. To honour these bonds, I approached my co-authors with the opportunity to story our lived experiences as Black women early childhood educators in Fort Worth, Texas from 2020 to 2022. Walking in the spirit of my foremothers, I wanted to go beyond the confines of traditional narrative inquiry and to write authentically and bravely.

The purpose of this book was to provide a space for Black women early childhood educators' 'specialized bodies of knowledge' (Dillard, 2000, p. 664) that is often underappreciated in academic literature on teachers' lived experiences. Instead of simply presenting my interpretations as a researcher of these women's lives, the authors provided self-defined understandings of their pedagogical stances based on their experiences. Each of the chapters presented in this book represents a Black woman educator's truth. Black feminist thought allows us to examine how Black women manage the everyday tasks of life despite the challenging situations we find ourselves in. Our knowledge may or may not be the result of formal avenues of education. Our communal funds of knowledge could even be understood as preferential (Acosta, 2019; Lindsay-Dennis, 2015; Walker, 1983).

Black Feminist Thought

As the 19th century ended and the 20th century emerged, Black women pushed forward towards defining our version of womanhood (Giddings, 2001). The formation of clubs for Black women was less about fitting neatly into white women's previously conceived notion of femininity and more about acknowledging the necessity of an exclusive affinity space (Collins, 2000; Giddings, 2001). By the mid-20th century, Black women created and sustained powerful social justice activist organizations, such as the National Council of Negro Women, for decades. Although Black women held some positions of power during the Civil Rights Movement of the 1950s and 1960s, the undercurrent of sexism within this liberation movement was ever present (Collins, 2000; Davis, 1981; Giddings, 2001; Smith, 1979; Wallace, 1982). From strategizing with political leaders to physically supporting and caring for their comrades to standing on the frontlines during protest efforts, Black women's contributions to the Civil Rights movement are immeasurable.

These contributions set the stage for the creation of a new formal school of thought. A school of thought that centred the needs and lived experiences of Black women. A school of thought that, as Audre Lorde (1984) eloquently expressed, would help to channel Black women's feelings about existing in a world 'which hates our very existence outside of its service' (p. 122). Collins (2000) examined the following tenets of Black feminist thought: (a) an understanding of the connection between experience and consciousness; (b) a legacy of struggle; (c) self-defined standpoint fostered by experience; (d) essential merger of intellectual work and activism; (e) recognition of changing dynamics; and (f) a commitment to universal struggles against oppression. Black feminist thought filled the echo chamber of critical social theory by providing a context for a liberation movement that was centred around multiple sites of oppression: (a) race, (b) gender, (c) sexual orientation, and (d) class.

The Combahee River Collective was founded in 1974 by a group of radical Black feminists, including Barbara Smith, Beverly Smith, and Demita Frazier (Taylor, 2019). The essence of the Combahee River Collective's (1982) argument was that Black girls become aware of the impact of their gender on their experiences within their communities as a rite of passage. This shared consciousness developed because of similar experiences. Black feminist thought promotes the consideration of how thoughts shape one's actions (Collins, 2000). As Black women critically self-reflect on our place in the world around us, we come to appreciate the beauty provided by the range of our experiences as well as the power embedded in the common threads of our existence (Smith, 1979).

Crenshaw et al. (1995) defined intersectionality as 'the various ways in which race and gender interact to shape the multiple dimensions' of Black women's social and political lives (p. 1244). Intersectionality seeks to provide space for overlapping of experiences in American society. What happens when a Black woman must consider her race and gender when engaging with systems of oppression? How does her sexual identity or religious affiliation affect how others interact with her? When the civil rights of a racial group are seen as a broad, single issue as opposed to a complex spider web of entangled familiarities, the unique needs of the most disregarded individuals get taken for granted and unaddressed (Crenshaw, 1991). Delgado and Stefancic (2001) asserted that intersectionality and anti-essentialism serve as the mirrors that critical race theorists use to look inward and critically '[examine] the interplay of power and authority within minority communities and movements' (p. 51).

Importance of the Current Work

Researchers have found that Black women educators' counter-narratives often included the following themes: (a) teaching as a lifestyle and a public service, (b) discipline as expectations for excellence, (c) teaching as othermothering, (d) relationship building, and (e) race, class, and gender awareness (Beauboeuf-Lafontant, 2002, 2005; Case, 1997; Casey, 1993; Cook & Dixson, 2013; Dillard, 2020, 2022; Dillard & Neal, 2020; Dingus, 2006; Dixson, 2003; Howell et al., 2019; Watson, 2017; Whyte & Delaney, 2023; Wynter-Hoyte et al., 2021). Educational researchers have employed critical theoretical perspectives to examine how intersecting social constructs such as race, class, gender, etc. contribute to the ways in which we educate children in the United States (Ladson-Billings, 1998). We must study hard in the present and learn the lessons meant for us to carry into our future as we reflect on how we have been impacted by our past.

I am a third-generation educator. My paternal grandmother and my mother educated thousands of students over their combined 80 years of teaching. The impact of their service to my south Louisiana community is longstanding. I have been an educator for almost 20 years. My teaching philosophy has been heavily shaped by my academic training as well as the realities of my lived experiences as a cis Black queer femme presenting being. It is from these sites of being and knowing that a 'passion of experience' emerges as hooks (1994, p. 91) suggested. In addition, hooks described this notion of the privilege of having gone through the things that one seeks to offer an opinion on. This idea exists between the concepts of essentialism and anti-essentialism. I identify as a cisgender Black woman. This does not mean that my experiences speak to the experiences of all Black women. How we bring ourselves into educational settings as educators is influenced by several factors.

The authors in *Daughters of (Re)Imagined Early Childhood Education* explored the intersections of these factors through counter-narratives (Pérez, 2017). Ladson-Billings (2009) described how Black women are often type-cast as mammies, sapphires, and jezebels in popular film representations and went on to explain how these socially constructed misrepresentations are connected to the lack of counter-narratives about the lived experiences of Black women teachers in academic literature. How we see ourselves in relation to our students and the world around us influences how we connect with those students. Reflective practitioners take the time to consider how their actions contribute to the outcomes of their work. This critical self-reflection often prompts some form of dynamic change as the educator begins to understand how they bring themselves into their classrooms and how the intersections of their identity impact their efficacy as teachers. Narrative inquirers maintain that simply analyzing the numbers through quantitative methods fails to fully capture the essence of what occurs across time and space in educational settings (Connelly & Clandinin, 1990; Craig, 2011; Kim, 2016). Cook and Dixson (2013) affirmed the power of considering contextual factors in narrative inquiry while crafting composite counter-stories based on the narratives provided by Black educators in New Orleans post-Hurricane Katrina.

Endarkening Narrative Research

Telling Black women's stories requires epistemological and methodological shifts towards critical social theories, such as *endarkened feminist epistemology*, that '…transmit necessary information, encourage dialogue, and maximize possibilities for the co-creation of knowledge' (Davis, 2015, p. 155). Dillard (2000) formulated the concept of endarkened feminist epistemology, defined as the articulation of:

> How reality is known when based in the historical roots of Black feminist thought, embodying a distinguishable difference in cultural standpoint, located in the intersection/overlap of the culturally constructed socializations of race, gender, and other identities and the historical and contemporary contexts of oppressions and resistance for African American women. (p. 662)

This book offers seven Black women early childhood educators' counter-narratives in our own words. Guided by the tenets of Black feminist thought and endarkened feminist epistemology, *Daughters of (Re)Imagined Early Childhood Education* approached narrative inquiry through a culturally situated lens that centres Black women's ways of being and knowing (McClish-Boyd & Bhattacharya, 2021, 2023; Turner, 2024).

Voices of Black Women Educators: Outline of Chapters

Our voices are central to the spirit of the present work as our stories are a collection of life notes (Dillard, 2000) – narrative representations that can be understood as 'embodying the meaning and reflections that consciously attend to a whole life as it is embedded in sociocultural contexts and communities of affinity' (p. 664). Each counter-narrative or life note was based on the author's responses to the following provocations.

- Describe what you were doing when the COVID-19 pandemic first hit Texas in March/April 2020. Feel free to write about in school out and of school occurrences.
- What were your experiences as a teacher like during the 2020–2021 and 2021–2022 school years?
- What was it like teaching during the pandemic?
- Describe your reaction to the murder of George Floyd in May 2020 and the subsequent Black Lives Matter protests during the summer of 2020.
- How were you impacted by the heightened focus on racial justice across the United States at this time?

As authors developed their life notes, we met on Zoom individually and collectively to discuss how our stories were emerging. These collective gatherings, or sister circles (Neal-Barnett et al., 2011), served as our support system during the writing and editing process. We often discussed our hopes for this project and exchanged words of encouragement. Our informal gatherings inspired the types of storytelling experiences that provide listeners with the ability to 'open their hearts as well as their minds and listen attentively to stories that feel raw, cut deep, and resist distance and abstraction' (Bochner & Riggs, 2014, p. 206).

To exemplify the traditions of Black feminist thought and endarkened feminist epistemology, I made the editorial decision to structure the counter-narratives in ways that captured the multifaceted layers of the mosaic that is Black women's lives across time and space (Evans-Winters, 2019) – boldly pushing back against the dominant discourse in academic literature. The reader will notice that the counter-narratives are intentionally written in an informal and conversational tone to 'literally [put] ourselves and our understandings of Black identities, notions of Black womanhood, and culture in the world in new and fuller ways' (Dillard, 2016, p. 411) as an act of (re)presenting our realities. Our life notes were grounded in the relational aspects of a Black/African-centred womanist onto-epistemology (Evans-Winters, 2019). Because each counter-narrative is meant to feel like a dialogue with a close friend, I subsequently refer to the authors by their first names to honour our relationships and sisterhood.

Each chapter in this volume begins with a brief introduction about the main threads of the life note. In Chapter 1, 'Letting Go to Grow', Bobbi begins by exploring how her relationships with her loved ones have shaped how she envisioned her role as a Black woman in early childhood education. She illuminates how the connections between her growth as a mother, daughter, sister, and partner have impacted her understanding of her responsibility to justice and equity as an educator. Myah continues this introspective look into how Black women process our emotions during chaotic times in Chapter 2, 'Shifting and Blooming'. Her story spotlights Black women educators' need for reflective spaces and quiet moments to ponder what moves one should make next.

The next two chapters of *Daughters of (Re)Imagined Early Childhood Education* shift to the theme of spirituality and testimony. Culturally situated narrative inquirers engaged in *endarkened narrative inquiry* (McClish-Boyd & Bhattacharya, 2021, 2023) and *endarkened feminist narrative* (Turner, 2024) have noted how Black women's narratives are often characterized by an underlying spiritual refrain. In Chapter 3, 'Destiny Detours', Krys details her experiences as a multiracial Black woman in north Texas and as a mother of two daughters. She expounds on her passion for special education and her desire to follow the meanders and bends of her faith. After ruminating on the unexpected junctions in her life, Alexis resolved that she had endured certain difficulties for a grander purpose. Her spirituality guides Chapter 4, 'Unsolicited Favour' and unearths a parable that centres the value of sitting still in the valley as we wait for what comes next.

The final three chapters of the text provide lessons on the complexities Black women educators face balancing the task of saving our own lives while caring for those around us. As we juggle the day-to-day expectations and generations of compassionate protection, how are we venerating the divinity that resides inside of us (Dillard, 2022)? Carson begins this conversation with an honest memory of her maternal grandfather and the impact of stigmas around mental health have had on Black communities. In Chapter 5, 'Question Everything, Always Speak Up', she describes how her first encounters with misogynoir occurred in her home as a Black girl. Stress tends to create situations where choices seem unfathomable – you struggle to maintain your composure while grasping tightly onto what used to be. Deidra chronicles what it was like to care for multiple generations and teach first grade during the COVID-19 pandemic in Chapter 6, 'A New Respect'. She shares her battles with anxiety and advances the narratives we have on how Black women educators continued to (re)create images of resiliency during vexing seasons. Chapter 7, 'Rock Steady: An Autoethnography Exploring My Lived Experiences During Dual Pandemics' is grounded in two of the fundamental principles of Black feminist thought – (a) the understanding of the connection between experience and consciousness and (b) the development of Black women's self-defined standpoints based on our experiences. In the closing chapter, I present my love letter to the Black women educators who simultaneously helped me mourn life as we knew it and celebrate the opportunity to nurture our wildest freedom dreams.

When asked to define caring in relation to students, Bass (2012) found that Black women educational leaders often used phrases that signalled a mothering and/or othermothering demeanour. Participants in her qualitative study discussed how their commitment to Black and Brown children extended beyond their regard for their personal well-being. Black women educational leaders exemplified this ethic of risk (Bass, 2012) through their actions before, during, and after the school day. The authors in this volume also demonstrated this communal ethic of caring (Green, 2023) throughout their interactions with children and families during the COVID-19 pandemic. Each story in *Daughters of (Re)Imagined Early Childhood Education: Reflective Narratives of Black Women Educators in Texas During COVID-19* matters and provides insight into how each of us makes meaning of the world. In this sense, the chapter authors' stories work together to seamlessly illustrate the synergy provided by an intersectional critique whereby one considers how multiple sites of identity shape lived experiences and foster our hopes for a radical future.

REFERENCES

Acosta, M. M. (2019). The paradox of pedagogical excellence among exemplary Black women educators. *Journal of Teacher Education, 70*(1), 26–38.

Aiello, T. (Ed.) (2023). *The Routledge history of police brutality in America.* Routledge.

Bass, L. (2012). When care trumps justice: The operationalization of Black feminist caring in educational leadership. *International Journal of Qualitative Studies in Education (QSE), 25*(1), 73–87.

Beauboeuf-Lafontant, T. (2002). A womanist experience of caring: Understanding the pedagogy of exemplary Black women teachers. *Urban Education, 34*(1), 71–86. https://doi.org/10.1023/A:1014497228517

Beauboeuf-Lafontant, T. (2005). Womanist lessons for reinventing teaching. *Journal of Teacher Education, 56*(5), 436–445. https://doi.org/10.1177/0022487105282576

Bochner, A. P., & Riggs, N. A. (2014). Practicing narrative inquiry. *The Oxford Handbook of Qualitative Research,* 194–222. https://doi.org/10.1093/oxfordhb/9780199811755.013.024

Carruthers, C. (2018). *Unapologetic: A Black, queer, and feminist mandate for radical movements.* Beacon Press.

Case, K. (1997). African American othermothering in the urban elementary school. *The Urban Review, 29*(1), 25–39.

Casey, K. (1993). *I answer with my life: Life histories of women teachers working for social change.* Routledge.

Collins, P. H. (2000). *Black feminist thought: Knowledge, consciousness, and the politics of empowerment.* Routledge.

Combahee River Collective. (1982). A black feminist statement. In G. Hull, , P. B. Scott, , & B. Smith, (Eds.), *All the women are white, all the blacks are men, but some of us are brave* (pp. 13–22). The Feminist Press.

Connelly, F., & Clandinin, D. (1990). Stories of experience and narrative inquiry. *Educational Researcher, 19*(5), 2–14. http://www.jstor.org/stable/1176100

Cook, D. A., & Dixson, A. D. (2013). Writing critical race theory and method: A composite counterstory on the experiences of black teachers in New Orleans post-Katrina. *International Journal of Qualitative Studies in Education, 26*(10), 1238–1258. https://doi.org/10.1080/09518398.2012.731531

Craig, C. J. (2011). Narrative inquiry in teaching and teacher education. In J. Kitchen, D. Ciuffetelli Parker, D. Pushor (Eds.), *Narrative inquiries into curriculum making in teacher education* (Vol. 13, pp. 19–42). Emerald Group Publishing Limited. https://doi.org/10.1108/S1479-3687(2011)00000130005

Crenshaw, K. (1991). Mapping the margins: Intersectionality, identity politics, and violence against women of color. *Stanford Law Review, 43*(6), 1241–1299. https://doi.org/10.2307/1229039

Crenshaw, K., Gotanda, N., Peller, G., & Thomas, K. (1995). *Critical race theory: The key writings that formed the movement.* New Press.

Davis, A. Y. (1981). *Women, race, & class.* Random House.

Davis, A. M. (2015). Embodying Dillard's endarkened feminist epistemology. In V. E. Evans-Winters & B. Love (Eds.), *Black feminism in education* (pp. 151–160). Peter Lang.

Delgado, R., & Stefancic, J. (2001). *Critical race theory: An introduction.* New York University Press.

Dillard, C. (2000). The substance of things hoped for, the evidence of things not seen: Examining an endarkened feminist epistemology in educational research and leadership. *International Journal of Qualitative Studies in Education, 13*(6), 661–681. https://doi.org/10.1080/09518390050211565

Dillard, C. (2016). Turning the ships around: A case study of (re)membering as transnational endarkened feminist inquiry and praxis for Black teachers. *Educational Studies (Ames), 52*(5), 406–423. https://doi.org/10.1080/00131946.2016.1214916

Dillard, C. (2020). (Re)membering blackness, (re)membering home: Lessons for teachers from a primary school in Ghana, West Africa. *International Journal of Qualitative Studies in Education, 33*(7), 698–708. https://doi.org/10.1080/09518398.2020.1751893

Dillard, C. B. (2022). *The spirit of our work: Black women teachers (re)member.* Beacon Press.

Dillard, C. B., & Neal, A. (2020). I am because we are: (Re)membering Ubuntu in the pedagogy of Black women teachers from Africa to America and back again. *Theory into Practice, 59*(4), 370–378. https://doi.org/10.1080/00405841.2020.1773183

Dingus, J. (2006). Community reciprocity in the work of African-American teachers. *Teaching Education, 17*(3), 195–206.

Dixson, A. D. (2003). Let's do this. *Urban Education, 38*(2), 217–235. https://doi.org/10.1177/0042085902250482

Evans-Winters, V. E. (2019). *Black feminism in qualitative inquiry.* Routledge.

Giddings, P. (2001). *When and where i enter: The impact of Black women on race and sex in America.* Perennial.

Green, M. L. (2023). Building culturally situated relationships with BIPOC children through a communal ethic of care. *Early Childhood Education Journal, 52*(5), 935–948.

Hooks, B. (1994). *Teaching to transgress: Education as the practice of freedom.* Routledge.

Howell, D., Norris, A., & Williams, K. L. (2019). Towards Black gaze theory: How Black female teachers make Black students visible. *Urban Education Research and Policy Annuals, 6*(1), 20–30. https://core.ac.uk/download/pdf/229870441.pdf

Kim, J. (2016). *Understanding narrative inquiry.* Sage Publications.

Ladson-Billings, G. (1998). Just what is critical race theory and what's it doing in a nice field like education? *International Journal of Qualitative Studies in Education, 11*(1), 7–24. https://doi.org/10.1080/095183998236863

Ladson-Billings, G. (2009). 'Who you callin' nappy headed?' A critical race theory look at the construction of Black women. *Race, Ethnicity, and Education, 12*(1), 87–99. https://doi.org/10.1080/13613320802651012

Lindsay-Dennis, L. (2015). Black feminist-womanist research paradigm: Toward a culturally relevant research model focused on African American girls. *Journal of Black Studies, 46*(5), 506–520. https://doi.org/10.1177/0021934715583664

Lorde, A. (1984). *Sister outsider: Essays and speeches.* Crossing Press.

McClish-Boyd, K., & Bhattacharya, K. (2021). Endarkened narrative inquiry: A methodological framework constructed through improvisations. *International Journal of Qualitative Studies in Education, 34*(6), 534–548.

McClish-Boyd, K., & Bhattacharya, K. (2023). Methodological considerations for endarkened narrative inquiry. *Qualitative Inquiry.* https://doi.org/10.1177/10778004231186565

Neal-Barnett, S., Stadulis, R., Murray, M., Payne, M. R., Thomas, A., & Salley, B. B. (2011). Sister circles as a culturally relevant intervention for anxious Black women. *Clinical Psychology, 18*(3), 266–273. https://doi.org/10.1111/j.1468-2850.2011.01258.x

Pérez, M. S. (2017). Black feminist thought in early childhood studies: Re) centering marginalized feminist perspectives. In K. Smith, K. Alexander, S. Campbell (Eds.), *Feminism (s) in early childhood: Using feminist theories in research and practice* (pp. 49–62).

Smith, B. (1979). Toward a black feminist criticism. *Women's Studies International Quarterly, 2*, 183–194. https://doi.org/10.1016/S0148-0685(79)91780-9

Taylor, K. (2019). Black feminism and the Combahee river collective. *Monthly Review,* 1–19. https://doi.org/10.14452/mr-070-08-2019-01_2

Turner, C. R. (2024). Endarkened feminist narrative. In *Encyclopedia of social justice in education.* Bloomsbury Publishing.

Walker, A. (1983). *In search of our mothers' gardens: Womanist prose.* Harcourt Brace Jovanovich.

Wallace, M. (1982). A Black feminist's search for sisterhood. In A. G. T. Hull, P. B. Scott, & B. Smith (Eds.), *All the women are white, all the blacks are men, but some of us are brave: Black women's studies* (pp. 5–12). The Feminist Press.

Watson, W. (2017). Educating in a 'regressive era': Exploring the race-full ideological standpoint of Black women teachers. *The Urban Review, 49*(2), 217–238. https://doi.org/10.1007/s11256-017-0398-9

Whyte, K. L., & Delaney, K. K. (2023). Exploring professionalization in early childhood: Reflections from a veteran Head Start teacher. *Contemporary Issues in Early Childhood, 1.* https://doi.org/10.1177/14639491231206001

Wynter-Hoyte, K., Thornton, N. A., Smith, M., & Jones, K. (2021). A revolutionary love story in teacher education and early childhood education. *Theory Into Practice, 60*(3), 265–278.

ADDITIONAL READING

Smith, B. (1982). Racism and women's studies. In A. G. T. Hull, P. B. Scott, & B. Smith (Eds.), *All the women are White, all the Blacks are men, but some of us are brave: Black women's studies* (pp. 48–51). The Feminist Press.

CHAPTER 1

LETTING GO TO GROW

Bobbi Reagor Marshall
The Kessler School, USA

ABSTRACT

Our relationships with those closest to us form the foundation of how we move in the world. Black women educators often curate relationships with their students that model the care and concern we want shown to our loved ones. Bobbi's story echoes this desire to be the kind of early childhood educator that her son and daughter would be proud of. In this chapter, she shares how her journey towards becoming the best version of herself was built on her passion for advocating for the well-being of the people she loved most and trusting in the process of growth.

Keywords: Family relationships; personal growth; self-advocacy; parenting and education; community building; empathy in teaching

INTRODUCTION

When someone asks to define me, I often ponder for a while on that question. Who am I, really? Does anyone know how to answer that question? I typically answer, 'Should I begin with whom I imagined I would be, or whom I am becoming?' I grew up in Dallas, Texas with my mom and stepdad. My parents worked hard, but they worked for corporate America. I remember an abundance of conversations I would have with my mom surrounding career choices. She would say to me, 'Please do not get a job working in a little cubical area where no one appreciates what you do. Go to school, study something that you know the world will always need, and make sure you are happy!' I did not quite understand that as a middle school student, but I did know what it felt like to be underappreciated for your hard work.

I do not have a close relationship with my dad. This is due to the choices he has made to be in and out of my life. Now that I have a family, I'm more protective of myself and my kids. When we were close, our conversations would intel the secrets to surviving the work world, facing challenges, reaping those rewards, and retiring early. As I look back on what he has done for me, I learned how to work through heartache, work through trusting others, and learn that regardless of someone being family, they aren't always fit to be in your life. That can be a hard pill to swallow when it's your mom or dad. Now that I am married to my amazing husband, he has shown me through my daughter how a dad is supposed to have a relationship with his daughter.

My mom yearned for me to be successful, but if it were my choice, being an educator was not in my future. My mom often told my sister and I to 'find a job in education or the medical field, because those are two careers that will never go away'. I wanted to find a good job, make money, mind my business, and repeat. I took a few courses in anatomy and physiology which made me anxious and full of doubt. So, I embarked on a career in teaching, and it has been the challenging and rewarding place that my mom always wanted for me. When I have conversations with my kids about careers, I simply tell them, 'The important thing is for you to be happy in what you do. Just remember your morals, and values, and always advocate for yourself and others'.

Figure 1.1 below is a depiction of my state of teaching. It describes the excitement, passion, and purpose-driven teacher I am today. It also shines a light on my reality and how I feel about the many fears that come with being an educator and strongly sticking to my roots. I now teach at a private school and for the first semester I felt like I needed to prove myself more than I had ever needed to previously. Why do you ask? Well, I am the only Black girl on our team. I'm the only Black girl that works on our floor. I am one of two Black girls in the entire building. So, to attempt to describe how I feel in this photo is only just a glimpse into my day-to-day as a Black educator.

COVID-19 PANDEMIC AND TEACHING

My initial thoughts on the COVID-19 pandemic, the rising of police brutality, and school shootings were that the world was coming to an end in the next second, and we had no time left to get this thing called life right. I was sinking, fast, and felt I could no longer protect my family from what the

Letting Go to Grow • **3**

Figure 1.1 The only Black girl. From the token Black friend: You're not the ally you think you are, by T. Warburton, 2021, https://www.queensjournal.ca/the-token-black-friend/. Copyright 2021 by T. Warburton.

world had done. As this plague began to strike our nation, it became more difficult for me to believe that we were going to be ok. A week after spring break, those who had travelled and participated in social events began to receive emails and newsbreak announcements on an upper respiratory infection that spread faster than a common cold.

Teachers received emails that schools were closed for another week or two, and we came back to take precautions. Those emails quickly turned to resources on how to stay safe during a pandemic. Panic struck as the word 'quarantine' rose out of the shadows and we all braced ourselves for the worst. My birthday was a few weeks away and I wanted to celebrate big, as this was my 30th and you approach this milestone of age only once. Well, like many other meetings, my birthday was celebrated through Zoom. I had never heard of this before the pandemic because my entire life was spent physically socializing with people.

In April 2020, we began planning how to teach pre-kindergarten students online. I laughed at the thought of a group of 15–25 4-year-olds participating in online learning. It was not ideal, but we made it happen the best we could. I think back on those moments and realized how many students needed to learn inside of a building with friends and teachers. The new online teaching was filled with distractions that sabotaged learning opportunities and focused on real-life problems to give children and their families real-life solutions.

Upon returning to the classrooms in the fall, every student and teacher was behind masks, fear, and the daunting thought of contracting a virus that was out of anyone's control. Materials could no longer be shared; hugs could no longer be given; and students could no longer experience what it was like to have fun in class and be kids. Social-emotional learning was then placed at an even higher priority, where teachers had to relearn how to deliver responses to behaviours. As child suicide rocketed at an alarming rate, kids were being left behind to figure things out on their own, because the adults in their lives did not have the answers and could barely help themselves.

The U.S. Department of Education stated that data collected before and during the COVID-19 pandemic showed that

> … in-person learning, on the whole, leads to better academic outcomes, greater levels of student engagement, higher rates of attendance, and better social and emotional well-being, and ensures access to critical school services and extracurricular activities when compared to remote learning (U.S. Department of Education, n.d)

We knew remote learning would be a disaster, especially for our students who longed for the physical classroom. Our students needed more than support in engagement and perfect attendance awards when we came back to the classroom. They needed adults to be honest about this hardship, but willing to break away from fear and create a new approach to learning and self-care.

By the 2021–2022 school year, I felt like I had gotten a grasp on how to move around without allowing negativity to affect my life. My kids though—my kids were struggling, unhappy, nervous, and overwhelmed. My son had fallen behind and was using the phrases, 'I can't do this. Mommy, I hate school now'. He was always tired and never had any energy for anything else that he enjoyed. He started to become a different person and I despised COVID-19 and many other things that had been going on in the world. My daughter was never exposed to formal early education because of the pandemic. So, she started kindergarten, and it seemed as though her teacher forgot that none of her students had previously had the opportunity to attend preschool. I blamed my personal experience with people lacking the ability to observe the problem and tackle it instead of sweeping it under the rug.

I began working hard at finding solutions for my kids. One thing that struck me was my Black child saying he can't do this. I never wanted him to feel so disappointed in himself at the age of 7 when the only thing he should have been worried about was learning how to ride a bike without training wheels. I reached out to the school counsellor and the inclusion team. I stressed the fact that we would not allow the school to let our children fall behind and after many children experienced tragic losses, the school needed to move in a way that supported social and emotional well-being first. I suggested more time to decompress before morning work and more time to build relationships with their peers. Overall, I advocated for creating an inviting environment that allows students to be productive in what they know and then gain the confidence to want to know more.

RACIAL JUSTICE IN TEXAS

Along with the fear of my kids losing confidence, something more unpredictable was happening in our country. The thought of my kids not being able to walk to the corner store when they are older to buy Takis and a Twix and make it back home without being killed by the very people that are supposed to protect them haunted me. I was reminded of the incident in 2012, when a 17-year-old Black boy named Trayvon Martin was shot and killed by former police officer George Zimmerman. This raised my awareness on gun violence regarding police officers. The death of George Floyd in 2020 struck a nerve that I've never experienced before, however. It struck conversations at home that many parents wanted to avoid. I felt the same. As I sat to try and find the words to describe to my kids what had happened, I simply said, 'police are supposed to be the good guys'. My son responded with, 'so who are we supposed to call now?'

I attended my first protest in Dallas. As beautiful as it looked, it was quite intimidating to see so many law enforcement officers lined up waiting for anyone to make the wrong move. The wrong move could have very well just been us walking down the street. Were they there to protect us or themselves? This moment made me look back to when I was 17, in an abusive relationship with someone who almost took my life. At the time, it felt like innocent people get treated the worst. My abuser went to jail for a moment, but it had nothing to do with mistreatment of women. Instead, he translated his impulsive and bullying ways into starting his own business as a tattoo artist with his own shop. George Floyd and many others did not deserve to die at the hands of someone else. Just like those innocent people, I could relate to them and how they are treated like an existing body that holds no morals to anyone or intent in this world.

I didn't know how to feel with all these things going on. When the Black Lives Matter (BLM) movement started, I felt like we were right back where we started with having to be careful about going out and moving about the city. With COVID-19, the media said that masks will protect us. With the increase of murders by police officers, what did we have to protect ourselves? Let's actually reverse back to the BLM movement. When it was created, it had the right intentions. Everyone I knew was ready for a change and excited for people to hear our voices.

I sensed that the BLM Movement eventually changed and became another social media fab that would be taken over by people who have never had to face any hardship being born Black. I asked two women (referred to as T. Starghill and C. Spears), both wives and moms who aspire to do more for their community, about how they felt about the BLM movement and where they stand today. T. Starghill stated that she felt that:

> The BLM movement started with the right intentions but has morphed into a tagline that Republicans use to mock our attempts to progress in this country. This issue falls on our own people who abuse the movement for their power-driven financial gains. I do not need the organized BLM movement. My life is a BLM movement of its own. (personal communication, 2023)

Starghill made several major points, but one that stood out to me was her stating that she didn't need the movement, that she was a movement on her own. This enlightening statement drives me to take pride in being the only Black educator on my teaching team. C. Spears, another close friend of mine, describes her relationship with the BLM movement. She stated:

> It makes me mad, sad, and disgusted all at the same time. It brought focus to the issues that have been happening way before social media and cell phones. It also brought attention to what we all knew was happening. Politicians have turned it into another racial group with an agenda other than what it was created for. Even our own people use it as clout chasing. It's a reminder for those who don't care or who choose that we are people too and our lives have meaning. (personal communication, 2023)

On 6 January 2021, an attack on the White House following the defeat of the former president, Donald Trump, sent a message that would heighten the response to many Republicans. After the riot, which allegedly caused harm to many, security for the White House was quickly revamped and ready to be protected. The interesting thing is, as an educator I feel that we lack this type of security when people attack schools. Why is it that the White House can double up on security, but schools only have officers during morning and afternoon carlines for routine traffic stops? The United States has had 13 school shootings, and we are only 3 months into the year. In my opinion, everything is backward, money-driven, abusive, and heartbreaking.

My children at home typically face problems that I did not endure until I was in high school and old enough to understand how to respond. This past year, they have been called out about their skin colour just about every other month of the school year. My daughter came home one day and said she was climbing up the jungle gym and a group of boys said, 'Black girl alert'. She proceeded to ask me what they meant by that comment, and I will be honest, I did not know how to answer her question in a way that a seven-year-old would understand. No one will ever prepare you for how to raise children in a society that teaches them to hate themselves and others.

LESSONS LEARNED

Donald Glover, also known as Childish Gambino said it best—'This is America, don't catch you slippin' now' (Glover, 2018). Remember those commercials that would show hungry children in different countries and paint this picture that living in America is your best bet! I think that the situation is daunting to know that we are no longer selling the 'American Dream'. I remember when I wanted the white picket fence, but now all I need to do is simply survive the increase of cost in rent, car loans, food, and gas. It's a stuck feeling of being out of control on how I live my life. It's intimidating. I don't want to say that I've changed, but I refuse to let America define me.

Sometimes, I feel like I will always be underneath a glass ceiling. Just waiting and watching lives unfold in front of me. It reminds me of a sunflower a few years ago, and while the seasons changed and Texas weather did what it does best, it taught me a few things. It started as a tiny seed and grew to be about 4 feet tall. Its stem was strong, it grew several tiny flowers, and was a showstopper when people drove by. I related so much to this sunflower because not only did it go through immaculate weather changes and survive, but the stem had broken, and I had to cut the sunflower to regrow.

Last year during recess, a colleague of mine had fostered a child around the age of 5 or 6. My colleague is White, the little girl is Black. I remember she used to express how difficult it was to raise her but how much she adores loving her. One day, she said, 'Bobbi, I should send her to you because you know... you can relate!' My response was, 'Yeah she would probably be better off with someone who doesn't dangle her in people's faces like a new puppy'. She had been so proud of adopting a little Black girl and assuming she was giving her a better life. Once again, the perfect example of abuse of power and too much money she lost and didn't understand how thinking that way eventually hurts her Black child. Educating kids is easier than educating racist adults, but the key is to stay humble and stand your ground.

I must admit, I am drained and over being a classroom teacher. It is situations like the one described above that make me want to explore educating adults about the importance of building children's self-esteem. It's not about the latest fashions or allowing them to choose their breakfast or lunch for the day. I must also understand that while attempting to create a path for my students and my kids, this path was not created for everyone to succeed.

I've learned that my career in early education is rewarding, yet extremely problematic, underappreciated, just the low blow of education. I say this because I have witnessed the benefits in early learning and making connections with families regarding their children is the highlight of my career. The dark side is that I hardly have a voice in how I protect my students, curriculum usage, parent communication, and not to mention, living paycheck to paycheck. I have met many parents who definitely see early childhood education as a large group of babysitters. I have also been blessed with a group of parents and students who view early childhood education as the holy grail of education. I look at both groups as an opportunity to display the wealth and opportunities that arise from receiving early education.

I learned from my mom how to listen to my children when they want to talk. I did not have that opportunity as a child. Many of us know the whole 'stay in a child's place' comment. I think I would have been a better-behaved teenager had I known what was going on in my home and could have answered many questions I had but was not allowed to ask. Jeremiah and Jaedon may ask some of the most awkward and uncomfortable questions, but I will never tell them they aren't allowed to have an answer to that. We know that if we aren't honest with our children, they will go searching for the answers elsewhere and it may not be the safest place to look.

Like the sunflower, life has been rough, glorious, cutthroat, and heartfelt. I am learning to enjoy every moment, even if some moments seem to be dreadful. It's about taking those moments and making the best out of the tiny victories that arise beneath the surface. Growth, trial and error, failure, disappointment, and achievements. It's all a part of the life God granted us, it's what we do with these moments that really shape the person we want to become and who we are today.

REFERENCES

Glover, D. (2018). This is America. [Song]. *RCA*.

U.S. Department of Education. (n.d.). *Supporting students during the COVID-19 pandemic: Maximizing in-person learning and implementing effective practices for students in quarantine and isolation.* https://www.ed.gov/coronavirus/supporting-students-during-covid-19-pandemic

Warburton, T. (2021). The token black friend: You're not the ally you think you are. [Photograph]. *Queen's Journal.* https://www.queensjournal.ca/the-token-black-friend/

CHAPTER 2

SHIFTING AND BLOOMING

Myah Breaux
United to Learn, USA

ABSTRACT

As Black women educators sit in the messy spaces of racialized and gendered lived experiences, there are often periods of growth that test their resolve to persevere. These trials are characterized by opportunities to transform into more than one ever imagined possible. In this chapter, Myah documents the shifts she made as an early career educator through dual pandemics in north Texas. She builds her story around the ways in which her emotions have shaped how she moves in the world.

Keywords: Emotional resilience; self-compassion; self-reflection; teacher burnout; introspection; mental health

INTRODUCTION

I think of my life like the flowers in the photo above (see Figure 2.1). Like pretty much anyone else, who I am today is pretty much an amalgamation of the past 27 years of life I have lived. I was born and raised in the Pelican state, Louisiana. I always tell people, 'I'm a Louisiana girl through and through', with being born in Lafayette, raised in Alexandria, and then eventually moving to Baton Rouge to continue my education at Louisiana State University. Despite any trials I may have had, I think about living in

Figure 2.1 Colourful flowers in a field. Photo credit, Myah Breaux.

Louisiana as a time of comfort. Life growing up down south consisted of the four F's—family, friends, faith and food. That last one still acts as a method of binding me to those around me. I come from a culture that relies heavily on the support and love of a tight-knit family. If I could describe myself growing up, I would say I was very shy and very sensitive. Still, I loved everyone around me and had an innocence that should truly be reserved for all children. I think of the younger version of myself very fondly, and sometimes wish I could go back in time and just have a conversation with her.

Things were very simple once upon a time: go to school, make sure your grades were together, come home and eat a rice-based dish, wake up tomorrow and do it all over again. When things get crazy, I often think back to before the shift happened. When did I transition from a little carefree Black girl who didn't have a care in the world to someone who is so consciously aware of everything that surrounds me? Someone who is not only aware of how things affect me, but how things I do affect others. Both of these things ring true in so many ways, but especially within the context of being a Black woman. There have been so many times where I have looked back at the simplicity of life fondly, wishing that I could go back even for just five minutes. Hindsight is 20/20, right?

NOTHING WAS THE SAME

The first time I had ever heard of COVID-19 was around November of 2019. I was in Wal-Mart with a close friend looking at board games for a game night we had coming up. 'Have you been seeing the news about that virus?', she asked me. I hadn't. She explained it to me, and I admittedly just brushed it off at the time, not at all realizing the severity of it. In the following months, I continued to read and hear about it in the news. Looking back, I still do not believe that I fully understood the magnitude until March 2020.

I remember when everything regarding COVID-19 happened so vividly. It was spring break, and with it being my first year as an official teacher and second year of graduate school, I was absolutely feeling the stress of it all. I was so excited to just have a week to rest and recharge so that I could come back ready to tackle the final two and a half months of the school year. I had a planned trip to spend a few days in Houston with some friends since the rodeo was going on. Making that three-hour drive, I didn't have a care in the world. All I was concerned with was the fact that in just a few short hours, I would be with people that I loved and cared about filling up my cup. Little did I know, I was in for a rude awakening.

The day before we planned to go to the rodeo, we all received a 'Breaking News' notification on our phones. This was the day that we found out that school would be closed the following week. I remember feeling confused. Shortly after began the very slow sinking in of what exactly was going on. We were met with a fear that wouldn't leave us for a very long time, a fear that I sometimes still struggle with—the fear of the unknown.

For the remainder of the trip, we tiptoed around what was safe to do. We ultimately decided not to attend the rodeo. No matter what we came up with, it felt scary or like we were doing the wrong thing, another feeling that did not leave me for a while. When the trip ended, I returned home still with so many unanswered questions and nothing but time to let my mind go crazy since I had an extra week off of work. That week was extended again and again until the call was finally made that we would not be returning to teach in person for the remainder of the school year.

During this time, I truly experienced the complexity of emotions. Initially, once I was past the shock and confusion, I will admit that part of me was happy to have an extended break from work. As I previously mentioned, the school year, being my first one, had me at the point of feeling like I was drowning. Of course, that turned into nervousness the longer the break took. That turned into feeling like I was going crazy at times. Too much time on my hands with no sign of the end. As a matter of fact, this was only the beginning.

Like I said, while experiencing a wide range of emotions, fear was one that never left me. Worry. Anxiety. Just to name a few. The more I watched the news, the more I felt fear. So many people were getting infected, so many people were losing their lives. I felt fear for myself, my family, my friends, and just people in general. The fear settled in even deeper the first time someone I knew personally tested positive. I felt like my hands were tied, and there was nothing I could do other than sit in it and let the time pass. There was no sign of the end; everything felt endless.

Another headache began a few weeks later as we were trying to navigate what was next for the education system. There was a series of things put into place and then scrapped. This cycle continued for the remainder of the school year as we all just simply tried to figure it out. Figuring out how to coexist with this virus was becoming increasingly more difficult. I filmed countless videos of myself reading books and implementing literacy lessons, knowing that while some students would be tuning in and watching them, a good percentage of them would not be. I worried about the well-being of my students and their families as well. I battled questioning if what I was doing even mattered or would do any good, a feeling that, you guessed it, stuck.

I crawled towards the end of the school year, navigating from both the student and teacher perspective, as I was also in the process of working on my master's defence. When we made it to May, a whole new wave of emotions set in. I was processing grief in different forms. Grief of life as I once knew it, as things were slowly settling in. Grief that after putting in the work for two years, I wouldn't get the opportunity to formally walk across a stage as I received my degree. My emotions were taking a toll on me, only to have salt added to the wound with the death of George Floyd.

WHEN IT RAINS

For me, learning about this all feels like a blur. Unfortunately, this is a result of hearing so many similar stories. One that sticks with me most to this day is the death of Alton Sterling. In July of 2016, as I was going into my junior year at Louisiana State University, about 15 minutes from where I lived, Alton Sterling was killed by law enforcement in Baton Rouge, Louisiana. This served as a time where a piece of that innocence I mentioned earlier left me forever. It felt even more tangible because it happened within such close proximity to me. Growing up in the deep south, I was fully aware that while there was that 'Southern hospitality, everybody loves everybody' facade on the surface, there was also deep-rooted racism brewing underneath. Still, even with this preconceived knowledge, this *really* felt like it was in my backyard. It marked the end of so many parts of me. It was the beginning of me struggling with my faith (one of those pillars) which absolutely shook my world as I knew it. I could not grasp how those who identified as Christians could be so jaded on something so intensely tragic. It was the end of so many relationships, and I even had a boss at my job I worked at during the time make some racially charged comments, which marked the beginning of my transition out.

Coming back, George Floyd's murder caused all of those emotions to come flooding back. 'Here we go again. Black people simply trying to exist, losing their lives at the hands of law enforcement'. I thought. I remember the protests came shortly after. This was tricky because I was battling between wanting to attend to show my support, while also experiencing fear. Fear of being around so many people when this virus was still so prominent; fear for the safety of the people around me as there were threats being put out for those who attended. One of my most vivid memories as we drove by was being called the n-word by someone who drove by. Emotions were so high at this particular point in time that even now, three years later, it still sometimes feels difficult to process.

I am someone who is notably very in tune with my emotions. I feel deeply, and even when they make me uncomfortable, they don't *truly* make me uncomfortable. I embrace the beauty and complexity of them even when they are the most difficult. With that, the slew of emotions that came with the death of George Floyd was one that felt heavy even for me. It felt impossible to navigate on top of everything else. To name a few, I felt sad, angry, confused, and eventually numb; the emotions themselves being somewhat familiar while the root of them being what felt foreign. A pandemic and the emotions that came with that, nationwide coverage of a senseless death while having to navigate the ignorance of those around me surrounding it, on top of just the regular stressors of life was not exactly a recipe for joy.

I went through a wave of ups and downs following the death of George Floyd with the state of the climate in the weeks and months that followed. Between receiving empty texts from old friends who felt guilty, and going through the motions of feeling like I was fighting an endless battle when it came to COVID-19, I felt drained. I felt as though there was nothing left for me to give to anyone or anything. With this, and already feeling as though I was pouring from an empty cup, summer was over before I knew it, and I was back to trying to tackle what was about to become my new norm—virtual learning.

ADJUSTING

At the time, the concept of virtual learning was one that made me extremely nervous. Still, I went into it as optimistically as I could. I remember all of the trainings we had to go through and all of the new platforms that were put into place. It felt like my first year of teaching all over again, except different. As a self-proclaimed introvert, I never truly realized how much I took little things for granted, such as having in person meetings. My new normal of being social was conversing with my colleagues through a computer screen.

One thing that I can say about this time period was that it truly forced me out of my comfort zone, tested my creativity, and mentally pushed me in ways that I had never been pushed before. Teaching is not for the weak, but virtual learning was a different type of beast. This fact rang even more true considering the fact that I was a third-grade teacher. I couldn't even blame the kids. Of course, it was difficult for them to stay focused while trying to learn on a computer screen and of course they were bored. We were all forced to try to make lemonade out of lemons in this terrible situation.

Still, I found myself at a crossroads. As challenging as it was to execute virtual learning, when it came to the pandemic, I still was comfortable staying in my home. For one of the first times, I felt safe, or as close to safe as I could feel in that situation. This all came crashing down when we received the news that we would be returning back to teaching in person in October 2020. I remember this triggering a whole new layer of fear in me. Up until this point, I had the privilege that many did not have, which was being able to work at home; I was not an essential worker. I had seen stories of people who took all of the necessary precautions, done everything we were told to do to keep ourselves safe, and still contracted the virus because they were forced to go to work. I was afraid, especially given that I would be working with small children.

I remember emotions being very high on the zoom call where we were given this information. People were visibly angry and scared. Still, there wasn't much we could do. Schools were going back, and teachers were being thrown back into the classrooms. When the day finally came, it was weird. I greeted some coworkers I hadn't seen in about 6 months, and others I had never even met before, despite interacting with them every day. It was a strange phenomenon, everyone being together but not. We were all in the same building, but separate. Meetings had to be held in our own rooms via Zoom. Over time, I even realized that I didn't even know what some of them looked like because I had only seen them with a mask. Even now, as I write this, I feel as though I am unlocking memories that I forgot were there.

The year was filled with challenges. Professionally, to name a few, parents had the option of bringing their kids to school or keeping them virtual. As a result of this, I had a virtual class and an in-person class. My struggles always lay with feeling like my virtual students weren't getting the same experience. At the baseline, it just simply wasn't the same, but you had to also take into consideration things like connection issues, and them just not paying attention at all. You couldn't even blame the parents, as so many people were simply trying to do their best during this time. Still, this came with worries that some students would end up behind.

Some new norms we had to deal with were a modified recess schedule. Since everyone could not be outside at once due to Center for Disease Control and Prevention (CDC) protocols, we only had recess a couple of times per week. Students had to eat lunch in the classrooms, which made it feel like we never had a break. Specials teachers had to be in our classrooms, leaving us to find somewhere to go, often having to share an empty room with other team members, while socially distanced of course. This also put us in a headspace of feeling like we never got break time to ourselves. That, combined with the circumstances of the school year, truly took a mental toll on me during this time. A point where all I would've liked was time to sit alone and process the ten million things that were happening—that was the one thing I couldn't get.

Personally, I found myself constantly worried about people who looked like me, especially my family and those close to me. People who did not have the privilege of having jobs that allowed them to stay safely at home because food needed to be put on the table no matter what. I thought about people everywhere who may have been in a similar socioeconomic status, who just simply had no choice but to keep pushing forward. I thought about how this would directly impact Black communities and communities of colour. There were so many layers to this that my brain just could not process fast enough.

Already considering myself to be an introvert who seeks true processing time while dealing with something, I was tested to the max. As someone who feels things deeply, being overwhelmed is something that I still struggle with handling gracefully. It left me feeling as if my cup was completely empty, or close to it at any given time, which in turn left me feeling as if I was failing as an educator. If I don't feel fully myself, how can I give my all to students? And if I am feeling so drained and beat down by my job, how can I manage the ins and outs of my personal life? The year felt a bit like I had the choice to either sink or swim, and I was sinking rapidly. I had to truly learn how to manage my emotions and the things that I feel, and leaning into therapy was one of my saving graces during that time. As I reflect on that experience, it truly played an integral part in the way that I process and experience things to this day. I have had to learn that in extremely stressful situations, both personally and professionally, what you can't control, release.

Alongside the high levels of stress and anxiety, there were the emails. Every time we received a cryptic email informing us that either a staff member or student tested positive, my heart sank a little bit. Would I be next? In the weeks leading up to Thanksgiving break, we received a different type of email. This email informed us that due to positive cases, we would be conducting virtual learning for two weeks after, leaving us with one in person week between Thanksgiving and Christmas. We were told that this was to see if there would be a decline in cases after people travelled for the holiday. There was both relief and confusion. Relief that we would have extra time at home, but confusion towards wondering why we couldn't have just stayed virtual. We returned from the extended break and learned that there were just as many cases reported, which made me feel even more exasperated. It felt like a never-ending cycle that no one knew how to end.

The remainder of the year felt like going through the motions, with me just counting down the days until the school year ended. The second semester clearly was a race to the finish, as many of those memories feel distant and blurry. I just remember making it to May, to the last day of school and feeling like I could breathe a sigh of relief. 'We did it! We survived the school year!', I exclaimed. Little did I know that this excitement would be short-lived, with me contracting the virus towards the end of the summer, when it was finally almost time to go back to school. Just when I felt like I could breathe, the crippling anxiety came crashing back in. This was a constant back and forth for roughly the next year, navigating changing restrictions from the CDC at every turn.

GRASPING IT ALL

As I previously mentioned, my emotions and experiences are a large part of who I am. No matter how challenging or painful it may be, I try to leave most situations in life with reflection and the intention to process what there was to learn. When I think about my time in the classroom, I definitely think it has been a unique experience. When I think about who I was when I first got into the profession in 2018, when I was just starting my journey into independence and adulthood, the woman that I think about feels almost unrecognizable. Even still, she is me.

She is someone who, despite certain life experiences, walked into this new challenge that was teaching with the most optimism, ready to change the world. She is someone who, while having the best intentions, made many mistakes along the way, because just like the rest of us, she is human. While the past five years have been quite a journey with many ups and downs, I am grateful for it all. The relationships I have built, mistakes I have made, lessons I have learned, laughter I've shared, and everything in between. I have learned that much like emotions—life is beautifully complex. I have had some very high highs and some very low lows, but they have all moulded me into the Myah that stands before you today. I will leave you with this. If I could name my top three lessons that I have learned in the past three years, they are:

1. Things will not always go the way you plan. In fact, most of the time they don't. Learn to roll with the punches and keep it pushing.
    (I'm still working on this one.)

2. If you cannot change it, don't sweat it. There is literally no point in spending too much time dwelling on something that is locked in the past and you have no control over.
3. Give yourself grace. This one may sound simple, but it is so important. We are all just trying to figure it out.

CHAPTER 3

DESTINY DETOURS

Krystle Dior Armstrong
Grand Canyon University, USA

ABSTRACT

Through life's twists and turns, Black women educators often reach crossroads where it seems impossible to navigate difficult crossroads. Krys' story details her experiences as a mother and a special education teacher in north Texas. Grounded in poignant truths and unadulterated passion, Krys explores in this chapter what it means to confront the unknown and establish one's purpose after years of searching for something real.

Keywords: Motherhood; spiritual growth; multi-racial identity; inclusivity in education; empowerment; self-discovery

INTRODUCTION

My name is Krystle Dior Armstrong, but Krys will do just fine. I am from Fort Worth, TX, Funky Town as the culture here would say, where good eats, good laughs, and just good ole southern folks love to live and share life experiences with what we are BIG on—FAMILY! Speaking of family, I have two of the most beautiful, goofy, talented, smart daughters—Kharynten (KD/Cupcake), who is 12 years old and Tamryn (TT/Puddin), who is 9 years old. These two are what I like to call my little rich broke best friends. Their distinct personalities reflect many aspects of myself and serve as a gentle daily reminder to keep going on this journey we call life. God knew I needed them, and I will always be grateful that he chose me to be their mother. I am grounded when it comes to them. They are the pit of all my reasons WHY, and I must make them proud—not just the other way around.

Here are a few more details about me. I have worked with individuals with a variance of disabilities since I was a teen. What started as helping the elders at church, or my mother's hair salon, began to cultivate a deep passion I wouldn't discover for years to come. By the time I graduated from high school, I got a position working for a community-based youth and adult group home, and it was up from there. Years later, I started as a substitute for Fort Worth Independent School District and worked my way into a full-time teacher assistant role. That's where the magic began to unfold. Here I am now still in a teacher assistant role.

Over the last five years, I've had the opportunity to have my classroom, get some in-depth professional and personal coaching, professional development, and many opportunities to thrive in my areas of expertise and do what I love to do my way—not the conventional way. This is all thanks to my former campus director (principal) Chaneka Rich, who in short would say, 'God gave you a gift & you understood the assignment!' Before teaching at Uplift Ascend, I had never been in a space where being unapologetically me was accepted. Previously, I had to codeswitch my verbiage, tweak the cadence in my tone, and speak from a professional standpoint all the time. Heck, I even had to dress the part, and most days I was hot and very uncomfortable.

Figure 3.1 represents my self-identity. I choose this image because, although we cannot predict the course of events in life, we may act with

Figure 3.1 Washing my feet in a stream. Photo credit, Krys Armstrong.

faith and confidence knowing that God is always with us, even in the midst of uncertainty. Along with my belief in natural therapy and focussing myself to be in alignment, I also wash my feet in natural water sources when I go hiking as a symbolic act of purging myself of any toxins that might be impeding my ability to achieve my goals.

WE GOT NEXT: IMPACT OF COVID-19 ON OUR LIVES

Ok, so boom! COVID-19 had hit, and I was clueless about what was happening in the world around us. We were at Six Flags, a local amusement park, surrounded by hundreds of people and germs without masks because that was totally not a thing yet. While in line waiting to get on the Road Runner mini coaster (see Figure 3.2), Tamryn began to dance in the line and yelled out, 'Ayyeee- We Got Next!'. Ironically, we got next would be our soon-to-become reality. We were there minding our business when my boss suddenly sent an email about school closing and what work may or may not look like as they are still figuring things out due to COVID-19. Did I

Figure 3.2 Road runner mini coaster at Six Flags Over Texas. Photo credit, Krys Armstrong.

mention I don't watch live TV, the news, or hardly keep up with any current events other than my own? Yeah, I'm that girl. Still not moved by even that. I was like, 'Ayyeeeeeee extended break!' Little did I know how much my life was up for a scare in the coming months. My precious baby girl was the first one of us to get COVID-19—yeah, We Got NEXT!

We made it home after a full day of shenanigans at Six Flags. I took a closer look at the email sent from my boss along with several other emails from the school district and peers. My eyeballs were moving in a spiral motion, and my brain hadn't quite absorbed what was happening. I wasn't sure if I was more excited about this extended break or becoming anxious about all the unknown and uncertainty. The next day, the city was put under strict mandates, curfews, and a host of other restrictions, and now I'm starting to grasp what's going on. More details surrounding school closings and plans on what teaching would potentially look like for the fall came flooding in. It was all so bizarre! Spring 2020 was a blur. We were all trying to sort through the technical issues of navigating a new online school system and figuring out how to live life with limited resources, social interactions, and limited access to daily needs.

By Fall 2020, the online school system for teachers, in my opinion, had improved as far as our understanding and comfort with navigation, but for our students, it was a new gaming tool and way to socialize with friends. Teaching on this platform was a disaster and a disservice, primarily to students in special education, who require additional support, or have disabilities that impact their way of learning. What I witnessed most was students who had capabilities, logged on, were interactive to a degree, and tried to complete assignments, but just wanted to talk to Ms. Armstrong and tell me about their day. For the students I serviced with a lower functionality, it just was not an appropriate tool for them, Not being able to gauge their attention span made it extremely difficult for me to know when and how to modify their learning. My students mainly learned life skills lessons and how to make the most of their abilities. I modelled the lesson or task, adapted it to fit their needs, and then gave them time to finish it on their own. This way, I could keep track of their progress and identify areas of growth. Since many of them were unable to understand the concept on the other side of the computer screen, my previous teaching methods were ineffective in a virtual setting.

Students with visual, auditory, physical, or attention deficit disorders struggled the most during these online classes. Many students required one-on-one, hand-over-hand, or adaptive device support, which could not be provided in this manner. This form of learning did not provide the numerous modifications needed to accommodate students' learning needs. During our time of virtual learning, I either held long conversations with parents on what they could do at home to work with their kids, or just sat on the screen watching my students eat snacks while running around their houses. It was sad—just sad. Most days, I'd connect to a general education class and offer small group support there, where I was working and rendering services to prevent myself from getting depressed thinking about how those kids were suffering during this time, wishing there was more I could do.

From 2020, up until now, I have spent a great deal of time trying to close that learning gap for the special education students I service. Special education typically just means increased funding for schools. Based on my experiences as an educator, I believe that it's all a show. Even though some campuses claim that including students with identified disabilities in school events is a priority, special education programs have severe setbacks and are usually overlooked and undervalued. The staff turnover rate for special education teachers is significantly high as well. For this reason, some measures I have taken on my own volition have been to: (1) work one-on-one with students after school, online or scheduled at home; (2) request additional support from my campus administrators for my classroom; (3) educate other staff members on the importance of inclusiveness; (4) ensure that these students have the same access and opportunities as their peers; (5) have meetings with central office management about my students' classroom and campus-based needs; and (6) give guidance to families on how to apply for community resources such as free tutoring, discounted therapy, free counselling, free groceries, job referrals, and a host of other things that are accessible to them based on their needs and their students. I believe that by helping one, I can help many. I am confident that continuing to advocate for this population will one day yield results, change the way schools are run, and lead to opening up more resources and advantages for them. My outlook is HEART work, not HARD work!

Teaching during the pandemic was a pivotal time. A time of restructuring my approach and delivery methods, a time to reflect and figure out how this will work and how to keep it working online and in the classroom. What I discovered is that students have a better connection to their learning environment if they can relate to their teachers and feel comfortable in that space. At Ascend, I found a way to remain professional while still being me. It has worked! With my students both in special education and general education, we speak the same language and understand hand gestures as greetings. We also understand that certain looks I give mean, 'I'm ok. Leave me alone right now'. My principal, who I lovingly referred to as Boss Lady Rich, use to say this is a cultural campus; we come from all walks of life. This is the first time I have ever felt like I could be me and not have to hide my true identity. It just felt right teaching here. Teaching finally had a purpose behind my passion. I felt a sense of belonging and that began to spill over to my students. If they didn't understand something, they were no longer afraid to ask for help or embarrassed to receive help.

For students of Colour and with disabilities that is major because they are the ones who hardly ever speak up or have someone advocating for them. I found a way to educate them in a space where they saw me, respected me, and trusted me as Nannie (Aunt), a big sister, mom, or just that person they knew loved them enough to be patient with them. I had adapted to a way of connecting with people who aren't directly related to them, but the bond felt like family. I strive to meet them where they are and not put them in a box or force them to learn something they just don't understand. I truly tap into finding a way to help them grow right where they are, with what they can do, and maximize the skills they do have. This has been my method and approach. My goal is to get better so I can continue producing results for students who, under my guidance, grow and develop to be their greatest possible selves. Teaching during the pandemic helped me discover the importance of building positive healthy relationships with my students and how it connects to who I am as an individual.

RACIAL JUSTICE AND BEING SOMEWHERE IN BETWEEN

I recall the flood of posts on Facebook about the murder of George Floyd. The Black community was outraged and hurt by yet another senseless killing of an innocent Black person. I did not follow the story in its entirety. I was, however, reminded of the Trayvon Martin murder. Two Black men leaving a store, minding their own business, and never making it back home to their families. The details are vivid in both cases no matter what angle a person views it. These individuals were INNOCENT, and their murders cannot be justified. Watching these stories, among others, is frightening. Several of my classmates led the protest in downtown Fort Worth. I saw small children on the front line at times. I was even asked to come speak at one of the organized protests, but I made an excuse to not show up. I was ashamed, to be honest. I mean what could I say? What impact would I have? Hell, I don't even know how Black I am. Growing up, I learned about racism, my father being a cotton picker, the Million Man March, the protest Dr Martin Luther King led, the vision of Malcolm X, what Rosa Parks stood for, segregation in schools. Listening or watching any of that was hard and sometimes a bit confusing to me. I'm still learning about my blackness. Just like our kids today, my parents didn't introduce me to the foundational concepts of being Black. My interpretation of being Black was that we wore name-brand clothes that were bought from the trunk of somebody's car or a lady passing through the hood.

   I am multi-racial—my father is Black, and my mother is Hispanic and white. My parents' roles in our house were different. My mom was the breadwinner and made all the major decisions while my dad was a minister and had side hustle gigs like selling snacks or knockoff designer purses at my mom's hair salon. Neither of them taught us much about being Black, and the culture that came with it. My mom attended every Black event in the community and sometimes she and my dad would coordinate events. They did a small business Black expo for years, but she never spoke much about her history or what it's like being Hispanic. When school-wide events happened such as Hispanic Heritage Month or Black history month, I always felt displaced and limited my participation because I wondered, 'Where do I fit in?' My dad was a man of very few words. He was always there, but I did not see much leadership from him. My mom seemed to fulfil that role.

I was taught, instead, to live seemingly under the radar because I was mixed with good hair, light skin, and pretty eyes. My mom did not want me to be conceited or a statistic of mixed girls are better. As a multi-racial child who had no understanding of my culture, or beliefs, I became like a chameleon—I was whoever I blended in with, but never fully became a part of any one community. This became a hurdle in my life, especially once I got into the education field.

I struggled with having uncomfortable conversations or teaching lessons knowing that I would get asked questions I don't know how to deliver an answer to, especially because I'm still battling my racial mountains and trying to overcome that feeling of not belonging. I would have never thought we would be living in these times, as history is repeating itself. I have seen people of Colour falsely accused, tormented, and profiled because of the colour of their skin. Not just adults, but children too. It's happening in the community, in the schools, and in the workplace. The difference between then and now is media and technology. I cannot help but think, 'What if that was my brother, my son, my friend, and how it would affect me?' When I see some of my Black students walking home from school, I immediately stop to pray. I have even spoken to some parents about offering them a ride. I know that I cannot protect them from everything, not even my daughters of colour, but I darn sure try.

These realistic horror stories force educators to teach outside the box and encourage me to discover my roots and find a way to connect to these stories and my students. Students ask questions we may not always have the politically correct answer to, but I choose transparency rather than misguiding them or giving them false beliefs. Because I never want a kid, including my daughters, to grow up feeling what I felt. At the time, my parents did what they thought was best. My position as an educator and as a mother is believing that my students have a right to gain knowledge; clarity of understanding; a right to real, raw, unfiltered history; a right to know where they are, who they are, and why things around them happen. They need to know being Black is important, it's also beautiful!

DESTINY'S CHILD: LIFE LESSONS REVEALED

In the last 3 years, I have grown significantly professionally and personally. Let me tell you a short story that ends marvellously. There was once a little girl who was always told that she couldn't, but she always did. Some said she wasn't good enough when, in fact, she embodies more than enough. The ones that hated her most said she wasn't worth much when the reality was, she just carried her calling differently. She has spent years operating in what was uncomfortable to her until God said it's time to step up, step out, and move in a major way. Does this story sound familiar? Maybe it was you. Maybe it is you. Maybe you know somebody somewhere who fits the description. Well, I stopped by today to tell you that purpose has power, and it will confuse the enemy. See, folks don't like anything that looks better than them, but when God selects you, the image is intended for you to stand out. Y'all don't hear me. I spent so much time self-sabotaging, hiding, and being around folks who ain't growing, and I was getting nowhere fast. I was uncomfortable because I was not in the space where God could get to me. I had to stop looking at myself as a failure, and paralyzing my vision, because of my poor decisions and start seeing myself through his lens. A person often meets their seating on the road they took to avoid it. For many years, I ran from my divine seat. I am a product of God's design—it's unique to each individual. I've learned that even if being me contradicts who they think I ought to be, I am free to be who God created me to be. If you are not my creator, then you don't have the right to critique me. This is something I instill in my students, especially the children of Colour and with disabilities. Figure 3.3 below represents my reasons for growing.

Figure 3.3 Mother and daughters' laughter. Photo credit, Krys Armstrong.

Don't allow anyone to dictate your abilities or your purpose! I say all that to say this: I still have my classroom, but now have been offered the opportunity to fulfil the lead teacher role until they can hire a certified teacher. This transition is further allowing me the space to teach in my unique ways, learn and gather more skills as it relates to being in leadership, and allows me to weight out how much more time I want to operate in traditional educational settings before I start making plans towards moving into a different role. My dream was tainted early on about going to college. Throughout my life, I was an honor-roll student with rebel behaviour, to say the least. I quit college three times before I took it seriously. I am humble and more excited than I can articulate to announce that I am now a full-time online student at the largest Christian-based University in the world, Grand Canyon University. They awarded me a scholarship and flew me out on an all-expense paid trip to tour the campus and complete orientation. This is a life-altering experience, and I am so glad I took the time to discover ME during the pandemic. Now, I am living out my spoken and unspoken goals and dreams. I never thought I'd be in this place or space in my career or personal life. Just goes to show you how our destiny definitely detours sometimes!

CHAPTER 4

UNSOLICITED FAVOUR

Alexis E. Moore
Summer Creek Middle School, USA

ABSTRACT

Growth and transformation typically take place under strenuous conditions in dark places that seem devoid of the light we are sometimes accustomed to. Black women educators' testimonies of faith and sacred trust demonstrate their convictions and hope in what may not be seen but is definitely felt. In this chapter, Alexis provides her testimony regarding the power of sitting still, listening to your intuition, and trusting in a process of personal and professional development that was guided by her passion for healing herself and those around her.

Keywords: Personal growth; transformation; generational healing; self-awareness; spiritual journey; community impact

And he will be like a tree firmly planted [and fed] by streams of water, Which yields its fruit in its season; Its leaf does not wither; And in whatever he does, he prospers [and comes to maturity]. Psalm 1:3

I am planted but not buried.

The scripture and image above (see Figure 4.1) represent the importance of my faith during troubling times. Things were looking up, well I assumed they were. New mom, new home, 'happy' wife, and blessed with

Figure 4.1 Clipart image of being planted.

the opportunity to be in my desired position as a reading interventionist. I felt like life had finally turned a corner as I was expecting new beginnings and first adventures. I vividly remember sitting at a round table with colleagues preparing for the post spring break state testing. We had a solid plan in place ready to tackle once we returned. But it still never settles in my spirit the fact that as I walked out of the door preparing for spring vacation, feeling accomplished and confident, my life would change entirely. What I once knew as my life would be different and my career as an educator would never be the same.

The end of spring break arrived, and I was preparing to get back at it. It was Friday, 20 March 2020, and I remember driving on this dreary day, almost in a daze but unsure why. I was on my way to visit my parents when I received an alert from my district that communicated a cryptic message, outside of the exciting 'No School' blurb that is broadcasted over automated phone messages or scrolling on the bottom of the local news station due to inclement weather. This one was far different, and a little uncanny to say the least. The explicit message said, 'The Governor has declared a public health disaster in Texas, closing all schools through Friday, April 3. The state will review reopening at that time, depending on the status of the COVID-19 pandemic'. The message was not only disturbing, but it also brought on the fear of the unknown which. Previously, the nature of this epidemic was downplayed and treated insignificantly. This reality quickly changed once lives were deeply impacted, including my own.

It was a time where no one had the answers and brains were scattered in a state of panic, not to mention those near and far falling ill and dying in the hands of loved ones (and of course the doubtful health system). For the first time, my mind became consumed with life and death. News coverage, press conferences, political upheaval, and social media rumours were only a glimpse of what was to come. As I navigated through the new reality of this pandemic, my fight or flight mode was automatically turned on and would not turn off. We all moved as a society in doing what everyone else did, which felt like a safe haven. Societal tension over certain freedoms led to violence, protests, and unfortunately uncalled-for deaths. It seemed nearly impossible to see a light at the end, to the point that I would wake up with very little hope and uncertainty. With so many unanswered questions, I would rush to news sources and social media for answers because no one knew any of the facts. My light continued to dim as life during as looming era of uncertainty was overtaking me. In a time where I thought I was on top with a new home, new job and mastering being a full-time working mother, it was so bittersweet. Unfortunately, this was only a precursor to what was ahead—ultimately the turning point of my existence.

I recall history books describing such events that I believed would never occur in my day in age. German philosopher Karl Marx (1852) once stated that, 'History repeats itself, first as a tragedy, second as a farce' which sadly included COVID-19. It was uncertain how education would take place with this new way of learning. Of course, many decisions were made with little certainty as to what would be these innovative ways to reach students. Virtual learning, hybrid classroom settings, peer participation with social distancing via video calls and chats, and deciphering emotions on a student's face with a mask were now considered the new normal. Humorously, these terms were foreign before this era. Well, at least to me. My outlook on education only dove further into this deep hole of disaster that our public education system was already facing—especially towards children of colour. I wasn't a bit surprised by the response and outrage (sarcastically speaking) that the world exhibited when they explained what virtual learning would look like. Already, educators were deemed underpaid baby-sitters with summers off and without input into the educational system. Although I could rant about the rationale behind this distorted perception, words would not be enough to explain the amount of stress and dedication required in this profession.

What most would describe as the 'world shutting down' was an understatement. At this point, I was scrambling and certainly not sure what I was expecting for the next school year. Surely, I thought that I would be secure in my career at this point in my life, though I was sadly mistaken and perplexed to say the least. Amid everything that was already going on, I found myself officially unemployed because my position was given to another colleague. A plethora of thoughts escaped my mind as I contemplated what would be the best avenue for my family—along with maintaining my sanity. To be completely transparent, I felt alone when making these decisions for my household. I was unhappily married and struggling financially due to both of us being unemployed. Just expressing those very words is difficult for me. Roles and responsibilities within the marriage were skewed and if no one was going to take the leap, stagnation would be the result. I think we can all attest to the fact that many relationships were tried due to quarantine, but that still does not negate the fact this was just plain hard! Although there were some commonalities amongst us all, every situation was different. Tensions all over the world were high because everything was out of sorts, but I know for certain that love and light were definitely not on my radar. Sadly, discord was another new reality within my household.

I would find myself sitting in the dark of my closet for hours on end weeping not in hope, but out of fear. I prayed and wept; wept and prayed. I just wanted to hide under a rock and escape life all at once. Everything around me was falling apart, and to think that the anxiety wouldn't begin to set in, is an understatement. Unquestionably, our normal lives were now distant memories. Maneuvering as we pleased and interacting with those around us freely without fear of falling ill would take some adjustment. However, I couldn't allow this debilitating feeling to be my downfall. There were mouths to feed, and bills did not quit, so the search was on. I tried to figure out what to do, and I didn't know where to turn—merely due to fright. I thought maybe this was my turn to leave education and explore another profession. I mean, even though I was at a turning point in my career, I certainly wouldn't have minded a new journey, since I was starting over anyhow—although soon I realized these words would become a reality. The anxiety of it all was overwhelming just thinking about it. I applied for different positions, but I lacked the confidence about whether I could land a job and still have the passion to continue as an educator.

Finally, a call back, but not from where I was expecting. It was an urban charter school, which, coming from where I'm from, was really unheard of. I wasn't quite sure how to feel, aside from being apprehensive. Due to little expertise outside of the public-school setting, I was unsure what that transition looked like, but my faith was definitely bigger than my fears. The people seemed great, and I was optimistic about this new change, but there was still this feeling looming over me that I couldn't seem to shake. The feeling remains nameless, to this day. I just believe God was pushing me in a direction that required his trust outside of my will.

I soon realized that the educational system that we once knew was now foreign to everyone, despite your years of tenure. I remember the words 'essential worker' mentioned, and I thought, 'Do I have the capacity to be essential right now?' I didn't question my ability to do the job; I just was unsure if I was able to pour from an empty cup. Making what seemed like impossible modifications to what was already a system of ongoing mayhem and uncertainty, was now even more challenging. I was overwhelmed, and I wasn't able to steer through for good reason—at least I thought so. All was a blur, trying to focus on being an innovative educator but depleted with fear and frustration. I went with the flow of things, but I can't downplay the fact that I just was not motivated enough as an educator to stick around.

I subconsciously began to understand how much this crisis was affecting me mentally, physically, spiritually, and emotionally. I realized that what I was feeling was beyond me, in which 2020 resurfaced some dark truths that I fled from and avoided for years. As a Black woman, suffering in silence is the known coping mechanism and a form of weakness if shown otherwise, especially with anxiety and depression. Therapy has had a poor reputation amongst the Black community as being dependent upon a third party to help sort out emotional traumas and rooted issues which, in a way, made me feel like I was cheating on my ancestors for seeking help. Growing up in a Christian household, where anything besides God was of Satan himself, kept me in a headspace of bondage. I am a strong believer in my faith, but this created a wedge of trust between my family and I that did not allow my voice to be heard.

My traditional Christian parents operated in a way of doing what had to be done to stay afloat. You know, just making sure there was a roof over our heads, lights on, and food on the table. Conversations regarding feelings and emotions were not warranted as priority—especially with the onset of one ill parent. Once I started to recognize rooted traumas that had not been exposed, I expressed to my family that I was seeking counselling. It was frowned upon to say the least, but I was determined to be a better me. To emphasize, there were some childhood traumas dwelling within me that had never been dealt with or recognized until this point.

The very anxious eight-year-old girl resurfaced with a force that I thought had outgrown and buried the baggage. I was reminded of befriending the school nurse in second grade who would nurture my stomachache because something inside was triggering the emotion that further enabled the symptom. I was unaware of how this was affecting me at that age. Always sick, a feeling of panic and doom, and social anxiety that could in no way be normal, but I later found out that everything I was feeling was valid. My parents were at a loss, and all along, anxiety had peeked its head in my life. By age 11, my father's several illnesses during my adolescence were emotionally demanding. I sometimes joke about my second home being hospitals and my new friends were emergency medical technicians (EMTs) and fire rescue—similar to how I befriended the school nurse. The many hospitals, facilities, essential workers, corpses, beeping machines, and the various smells would overtake me for many days. At this age, I knew for sure that I wasn't supposed to be a first-hand witness to this, but there I was. I didn't realize until much later in my life that maturing quickly and taking on the role as a secondary caregiver before the age of 13 was not only traumatic in itself, but a signal that it was time for therapy.

I can't begin to express the feeling of being lonely, abandoned, and needing to be nurtured. I felt like I had lost both parents at the same time.

My dad, through no fault of his, left me. I was thankful that my dad was still there, but transparently, I couldn't have the dad that everyone else had. We couldn't do the normal things together that were so commonplace. My mom did the best she could while taking on a new role as a caregiver, on top of still being a wife, mother, and the sole breadwinner of our household. I became her partner in this, which when I look back now was not a healthy choice for me. This is not to say that I should have been excluded from the chaos, but it is to say I should have been better protected from it, but no fault of hers.

I remember going to school and engaging like my world wasn't falling apart. There were days I would attend school knowing my dad had just gone into cardiac arrest outside of the house while I walked to the bus stop. I remember rushing to leave my street so that no one would know that it was my house that had a paramedic sitting outside of it. I didn't want the questions or concerns because in my heart of hearts, no one would understand; I barely did. What was happening wasn't normal, but who would come to my rescue? I was operating in a stale state where having both parents still alive by the end of the day was truly my only goal.

Fortunately, therapy has enabled me to tap into my traumas, but I'm still unpacking some rooted truths—one that has been a blessing and a curse. The loosely used term has been mistaken for being over-dramatic, but I realized I am a *hypochondriac*, in other words, suffering from health anxiety. It was a blessing in disguise because I learned that many others were dealing with a similar issue since the start of the pandemic (yes, I was a faithful mask wearer!). I was too embarrassed to share and explain the constant fear of being sick or having a chronic disease because it was daunting, frustrating, and it enraged me that my mind could cause physical symptoms to rule my body, which was the curse. Thankfully, I have been able to see that this anxiety reverts back to eight-year-old Alexis in the nurse's office with a stomachache. Although I can't blame all of my anxieties stemming from the age of eight, which I believe began in my mother's womb, I have a better understanding of the anxiety's root cause. The fact that I had taken the first step towards freedom was an accomplishment in itself, but of course more had to change. The summer of 2020 would do that.

Along with the upheaval of the pandemic, one of many names was being crooned throughout the world from a place of pain: George Floyd. On 20 May 2020, media posts flashing daunting videos of Floyd pinned to the ground with a White officer's knee made their way around the world swiftly. I can't say that my initial response was out of an act of shock. Sadly, I scrolled past the posts, which seemed as if I had become accustomed to the agony. I was numb and speechless and found it difficult to digest. The question as to when this would stop was rhetorical. Riots, protests, and court hearings did not justify our pain. We are hurting. We deserve the same esteem, yet our voices are being silenced. We are being muzzled with pacifiers of bare minimum to keep quiet. We are bribed into bargains that rob us of our God-given freedom to speak and justify what is true. Dangerously, there are those among us who look like us, but are not for us. Not only are we up against the odds, but our people have also succumbed to the pain and pressure, and standing up is more so an inconvenience. In essence, we are implicitly biased to our own kind. If we can't break the curse of how we see each other, is it possible to break it amongst those who don't look like us? Our culture has divided itself with tension and ignorance due to the lack of knowledge in understanding the importance of why in regard to our race and culture it is vital but is merely being ignored. Is there hope in sight for our Black kings and queens that we educate every day with the responsibility that lies on our shoulders to teach that freedoms are our rights? How can we, when our history is being stripped from textbooks and libraries to keep our scholars in the dark regarding the origin of our culture? To say hope is near would be a stretch, but without hope, we have nothing, for it has gotten us this far.

It's nothing like the feeling of being judged in every moment. I can't stress the fact that this has gone completely beyond the colour of my skin, but my way of life, my upbringing, my ancestors, my gender, my intellect are all being judged. Hence, it doesn't matter my stature, experience, or education because I remain a target. I'm Black, and a Black woman at that. Black women continue to be seen as angry, entitled, aggressive, and opinionated. Others believe that our mouths should be shut with no voice. Not to mention the ridicule received for being a Black educator. While some may be intrigued (or fascinated with the fact that Black educators are capable of having intellect despite the stereotypical view of blacks being uneducated), my intellect is not measurable, for I am still capable of governing myself cordially despite the offence to the stereotypical view. I learned that I don't need validation to prove that I'm worthy enough, whilst it's also not my job to break the stereotypes that engulf a Black woman's image. Essentially, no matter how on top we are, we will continue to be looked upon as the few to succeed. George Floyd was only one of the few to stand as a reminder that we are not safe and I'm not sure we will ever be.

Where the usual nerves set in during the summer with anticipation of which scholars will be in your homeroom or what the classroom theme will be, this year was much heavier. The same question that kept whirling in my mind endlessly after George Floyd's death was, 'How can I face our future?' The question was growing louder as the new school year approached. The pandemic prevented connections from being made with scholars, which would further cause a rift in building trust and rapport. Just anticipating it all brought on further anxiety. How would I find the courage to educate our Black and Brown scholars about the notion of avoidance to address the obvious regarding George Floyd's death? Contrary to my mixed emotions, I did feel at ease walking into my new position and was grateful to be in a work environment that welcomed social justice and support for our culture, but how long would those feelings last?

As I virtually welcomed scholars back for the fall 2020 school year, I could feel a sense of hesitation and a loss of security, ultimately unsafe from the world in various ways because of the virus, police brutality, racial injustice, school shootings, and more. By observing the blank stares on new faces through computer screens, I felt a sense of awkwardness, which I'm sure we all shared equally. As I sat in my small office space within my home, staring into the screen with unengaged students—sleeping, snacking, playing video games, or the usual black screen—I remember asking myself, 'Alexis, what are you doing girl?' I felt so out of place and discombobulated with uncertainty and confusion on if I was even doing this correctly. Even with tenure, this was like learning a foreign language and feeling completely lost. I endured the many changes and gained a newfound flexibility that I wasn't aware that I could achieve, but I was tired. It was weird because it was a different type of fatigue. I had hit a point of just wanting to quit it all. Every role I was responsible for had become so heavy—being a wife had become forced, being a mother had become a chore, and being an educator had become discouraging (not to mention all of these new discoveries I was finding out about myself). I felt myself becoming physically unrecognizable where my thoughts had taken over from inside out. I knew I had to make a change, but where would my escape route be?

Three months had gone by, and I was wondering where to turn. I knew financially my family could not withstand the loss of income, but was it worth losing my sanity? 16 October 2020 was the day I decided to leave it all without a plan in place. I left teaching for 10 months and dreaded the thought of returning. Although I didn't know what life looked like unemployed with a dollar and not much of a dream, I was certain it was what I needed. I can't say that my decision was rash, for I had been contemplating for a while, but I never knew how or when to take this leap of true faith. In essence, I was tired of everything. I could feel myself falling into this realm of desperation and just wanted to feel better. But my apathetic mood was taking over. It wasn't fair to be unavailable to these kids when I truly did not have the capacity to provide them with what they needed, especially during this trying time. Although we were collectively in this state of transition and change, I had nothing left to give my students. I would be doing a disservice to myself and my scholars by forcing something that I had ultimately lost my passion for. On the other hand, I definitely wasn't myself, which was my cue to walk away from what I once desired.

As the new year of 2021 approached, I embarked on a new journey to stardom, literally all over again. I made subtle changes that became impactful for my well-being like changing my diet, exercising, meditating regularly, eliminating alcohol, and protecting my peace at all costs. I had no idea this is what God had set forth for me in the midst of chaos and disarray. I'll admit, it was a challenge because I now realized how out of alignment I was. My mind and body had not been operating as one, which explains the symptoms. I often took walks to observe and take in how grateful I was to be alive and well, but in the midst of my epiphany, chaos continued around me. This virus was running rampant. I was on the verge of losing my marriage. My father was becoming progressively more ill. I was still a new mom trying to figure it all out, and then the obvious, being unemployed. Again, aside from all of the mayhem, I felt a sense of peace and stillness. I was determined to stick to the subtle changes that would become life changers when it was all said and done. I had never challenged myself to remain consistent which allowed me to feel empowered as a Black woman. I was choosing better for me.

As I was continuing to embark on my journey of a much-needed hiatus, I was beginning to see some necessary changes within myself. However, it seemed like the more I dug deeper, the more everything else started to fall apart. I started to isolate myself when I often felt in a daze just trying to stay afloat. Without the routine of day-to-day life as an educator, I found myself trying to re-identify my purpose. Had I really been so accustomed to doing life subconsciously? I realized who I was outside of consuming my time with being a full-time educator, wife, and mother. I continued to seek counselling during this time where revelations and realizations were continuing to become a reality, but terrified at the thought of where my life was headed. So many questions consumed my mind on what my future entailed. Would I potentially be divorced and a single mother before the age of 30? Would I ever return to education? Did I make the right decision by leaving teaching behind? I couldn't grasp all of my thoughts and emotions at once, so I began to petition my concerns and anxieties into prayers. I created a prayer closet engulfed with affirmations, scriptures, and quotes. I would spend hours on end trusting and believing that although I had no idea where I was being led, all things would work together. Unbeknownst, it would all make sense soon.

Most Texans will tell you about the unforgettable *Snowmageddon of 2021*, also known as the tragic ice storm that was a nightmare for more than a few. Roads were impassable and thousands were out of power, including for me and my family. What only made matters worse was the morning of 17 February 2021 at 4:45 am. It all began to make sense as to why God was isolating me in his presence. This was the day that my father's 20 plus year battle with illness came to an end. Prior to his passing, he had been intubated for over a month and of course due to COVID-19, no visitors were allowed. What made matters worse was that I couldn't rush to the hospital to be by his side at the time of his death; the roads were atrocious. I still struggle with the fact that he suffered alone, and I was never able to say goodbye or even say I love you. Even to this day, I still can't feel the pain that occupies my heart with his passing. One thing I learned about grief is that it comes in waves and chapters. It affects you in ways that are hard to realize at the moment.

I would notice myself struggling to remember things, being present, very quiet, and no motivation; all normal responses, so I've learned. From the age of 11 years old, I feared the death of my father and I never knew when the day and time would occur, which explains why the anxiety has been such a stronghold for this long. It seems rather odd to say, but the last conversation between him and I was pleasant, loving, and insightful, despite us being at odds at the time. Though I wasn't aware it would be the last, I'm holding onto it. I'm grateful that despite him being alone, I know in my heart that I would not have been able to heal peacefully if I would have witnessed his death while at his worst. I'm joyous that my last memory of him was smiling with my daughter in the comfort of his home. Transparently, with all this happening I struggled with what was next and how to continue on the course of re-identifying me. Although I was out of sorts, the time and space of being hidden was my saving grace. What may have seemed like such a tragedy was the start to my new journey. I sometimes wonder how and why God goes about things, but I concur that's not for me to know. As scripture says in Romans 8:28 NIV, 'We know that all things work for the good of those who love him', and I lean on that.

Still wondering what all of this was for, there was one thing that was clear: I was meant to educate, in whatever capacity that looked like. With the passing of my father who admired my profession, I humbled myself and moved back into the classroom in July 2021. I'll admit this was a dreadful choice being that I wasn't necessarily in the right mind frame to educate and entertain scholars, but again, my faith was bigger than my fears. As much time as I had to reflect and rejuvenate, God was otherwise moving me in that direction. Some things we just don't understand and this I was struggling to figure out. Despite all that occurred, I was determined to fulfil the purpose set before me. In all honesty, I was anxious about the pandemic and returning to in-person teaching. I was at an all-time high of caution and apprehension, but I gave it my best to look past the reality and do what I knew how to do. Everything was very new and different, but I look back now and say that the year of 2021–2022 was one of my best teaching experiences. I pushed through the pain of grief, burdensome expectations that the classroom demanded, and the process of re-identifying myself. Having the opportunity to build connections and relationships with scholars felt inspiring and liberating and I was confident that this purpose was just for me. Scholars exhibited growth and gains that went beyond academics, which in turn increased their ability to express themselves socially and emotionally. Scholars appreciated the fact that I was able to understand and empathize with their struggles, which led to meaningful classroom discussions and accountability for all. Without a doubt I had dreaded returning to the classroom, but it turned out that I truly was enjoying the year of transition.

Although I was seeing the bright side again of my career, I was swiftly losing my grasp on my personal life. Though separation from my ex-husband eventually led to a nasty divorce and a new role as a single mom, it was uncertain, but expected. I didn't realize that I was navigating through day by day, requiring myself to give it all I had when turmoil was at my doorstep. There were days that I was so excited to head to work and painfully thought about having to return home, which is usually the opposite. While now trying to get re-acquainted as a full-time educator, I was now one with myself to continue on this journey. Yes, I was losing something, but what I gained far outweighed the losses.

I can't say that my career in education as a Black woman hasn't helped me navigate through this thing called life because it has taught me important lessons on how to be resilient. Teaching is a lifestyle, in which I don't know many professions that require you to be present, show up, and serve others as a passion and not a means for self-gain. In 'The Spirit of Our Work: Black Women Teachers (Re)member', Cynthia Dillard (2022) states that,

> As Black women teachers, we had all walked into our classrooms committed to loving the students who appeared before us and to embracing the diversity and brilliance of these students, whether we taught preschool children or adults. But we also came to (re)cognize that our work as teachers was not solely about learning and embracing the tenets of culturally relevant teaching, attending professional development on culturally sustained teaching, or marshaling other culturally based curriculum frameworks. It was about (re)claiming our *own* spirits and (re)membering the humanity and cultural traditions of Black women and people as a precursor to carrying out the deeper cultural and spiritual work of teaching that these frameworks *require*. (p. 14)

This quote resonated with me because without our profession and Black women's presence in the classroom, there would be little change. I'm sharing all this to show that I am determined to be the change. I am determined to be a Black woman that ends the cycles and refuses to ignore self-awareness. Seeking help has not only served to better myself, but to transform myself so that generational curses are not transferred to my children and the children I educate every day. Educators have a direct effect on the outcome of another's life based on our own morals, values, and standards. If I was raised from an upbringing that lacked compassion, nourishment, and affection and those traumas go untreated, it is likely that those generational curses would be projected upon the students I teach.

Although there is still an abundance of work to be done in our classrooms and communities, we must continue touching a soul one day at a time. In all transparency, I don't wake up every day ready for what this profession is going to toss my way, but I am now empowered to show up as myself, serve others, and embrace the journey. I am planted but not buried.

REFERENCES

Dillard, C. B. (2022). *The spirit of our work: Black women teachers (re)member.* Beacon Press.

Marx, K. (1852). Marx's "Eighteenth Brumaire". In *The Eighteenth Brumaire of Louis Bonaparte* (pp. 19–110). https://doi.org/10.2307/j.ctt18fs6hn.5

ADDITIONAL READING

Staff, Y. (n.d.). Psalms 1:3 and he will be like a tree firmly planted [and fed] by streams of water, which yields its fruit in its season; its leaf does not wither; and in whatever he does, he prospers [and comes to maturity]. Amplified bible (AMP): Download the bible app now. *YouVersion | The Bible App | Bible.com.* https://www.bible.com/bible/1588/psa.1.3

CHAPTER 5

QUESTION EVERYTHING, ALWAYS SPEAK UP

Carson B. Willis
University of Denver, USA

ABSTRACT

Duality exists at every corner for Black women educators in America, and racialized and gendered discrimination is often coupled with more than human expectations of performance and grace. In this chapter, Carson documents her journey towards learning the power of her voice while confronting the complexity of talking back to inequitable systems in education and mental health. Her story focuses on the stigmas associated with mental health diagnoses in Black communities and the impact of choosing a career path as a healer in hopes of disrupting harmful silences and advancing justice, equity, diversity, and inclusion.

Keywords: Mental health awareness; duality; family influence; representation; authenticity; self-care in teaching

INTRODUCTION

Figure 5.1 brings back memories of my childhood. The summer before I entered the fourth grade, I wanted to be president of the United States. Spending months at my grandparents' house, with Fox News and National

42 • Carson B. Willis

Figure 5.1 Carson's papa, her older sister, and Carson. Photo credit, Carson Willis.

Public Radio (NPR) a consistent hum in the background, the political ramblings found their way into my adolescent mind as a political project to start my career as a leader in the highest office. I made a glitter poster that read, 'Carson for President'. I cut out index cards with my political aspirations to hand out to my long list of constituents: my grandmother, my grandfather (papa), and my older sister. Standing outside in the Texas heat, I gave my two-minute speech on how I, a nine-year-old, could change the country and even the world. After my address ended, a prominent politician-like smile spread on my sweaty face, making my braids stick to the back of my neck, and I looked at my papa. I waited for him to shower me with adoration; instead, he said, 'I would never vote for you'. I looked down at the sprinkle of leftover glitter on my shoes. I tried to mask my tears by wiping the sweat off my forehead. I whispered in a voice that no politician would dare use on their campaign trail, 'Why?' After taking a swig from his Coors Light, a staple in his hand, he responded, 'Because you are the two worst things in this country, a woman and Black'.

This was my childhood. On my mom's side, there were only my grandparents, who, being a single mom, my mom relied on as a second set of eyes and financial support. My dad's side was from East Texas, and I never saw them consistently. Growing up in a majority-white suburb, my only Black influence came from my mom, sister, and grandparents. My prominent paternal figure, my papa, taught me how to find my voice while voicing his distaste for my primary identity markers, setting a theme of duality in my adolescence. My connection to my papa was contradictory; I stood against everything he stood for, which is how I found a platform to share my voice and opinions. While he yelled negativities about the Black man in America, he told me stories of growing up as a Black man in the 1940s and how his options and education were limited due to his race. While he spewed sexist comments, when my eldest sister died, he looked at me, a Black woman, and said, 'If anyone can get their family through something like this, you can'. He taught me that not everyone is how they seem, that maybe not all situations are Black and white and that you can make changes by asking questions and raising your voice. He kept a consistent mantra running through my head from as early as I can remember: 'Question everything, always speak up'. So, I did.

I wanted to know why my grandfather's mood would shift sometimes for weeks on end. I wanted to know why my mom could not get out of bed, sometimes for days, after having my little sister. I wanted to know why I, a Black girl towering over all my classmates, felt so different in my majority-White neighbourhood. But most of all, I wanted to know why no one in my family spoke of these inconsistencies—why it was seen but normalized and never brought up in conversation. As I grew up, built relationships, and gained knowledge, I realized that my family was not unique in this quirk. Still, other Black families had similar stories and normalizations of people crying out for help but none being given. In Black communities, mental health is not discussed often; even further, seeking mental help is seen as weak or something people do when they have money to burn. I have a family history of addiction, chronic depression, and bipolar disorder that is spoken about in hushed tones and seen as a stain on our family line. I have lost an uncle and a grandfather to mental illness. Throughout their lives, it never occurred to them to seek help, and it never occurred to anyone in my family to offer it. When I was looking for a Black therapist in high school, I could not find one because there was none in my area. When I took my first psychology class in high school, my dad was perplexed about how I would use that information in everyday life. The discussion of mental health within my community is progressing, but it is not where it needs to be to help people gain knowledge on mental illness. This led me to want to gain a doctorate in clinical psychology and start a career focusing on mental health; this foundation for my future career led me to become an educator.

Teaching fell into my lap by way of the non-profit called Teach for America. I was nominated by an organization I volunteered for in college, interviewed for the job, and took it to help pay for graduate school. It was the perfect fit for my life track; it gave me a break before getting my doctorate, and I got to follow in my mom's footsteps, who has been an educator for the past 15 years. My first year of teaching was in 2020, and this past academic year, 2023, was my last. My track was short, and walking into this step in my life, I knew it would be, due to my true career being in mental health, which is why I hoped that during my three years, I instilled in my scholars the desire to question everything and always speak up.

The photo in the beginning of my story is of my older sister, my papa, and myself. It describes how I feel as an educator because it is something in my past that I will always hold on to. Each gave me something of value that I brought into the classroom to show up for my scholars. My sister was to be loud and, most importantly, be yourself, no matter who was in the room or who was watching. My papa was to be a lifelong learner and, of course, to lead with my actions.

ABSOLUTELY NOTHING

In March 2020, my life was on an easy uphill climb, like hiking and seeing a patch of grass with the sun shining down, just a little bit in the distance, you remember you brought snacks and a special drink just for that moment, but you have a little bit more of a walk till you reach your primary destination. I was in my last year of undergrad; I had already secured a teaching job for when I graduated. I just had to get through one more semester of college; I just had to walk a little bit more till I reached my destination and was done with college. In March 2020, right when I went home for spring break, I had a plan; it involved the following:

1. Live it up in Mexico for the week on my girl's trip for spring break.
2. Party in my last semester as a college kid.
3. Maintain my grade point average (GPA) to graduate with honors that May.
4. Secure recommendations from my professors for PhD (I mean, I would be applying to graduate programs in a year and a half)
5. Party.... Party some more.

It was a solid plan; it would get me through the next couple of months before I had to be a real adult. It was my little walk before I could sit in the patch of grass with the sun shining on my face. Then everything came crashing down.

When I think of the COVID-19 lockdown, I think of nothing and having to wrap my brain around doing absolutely nothing. I went from taking 22 hours a semester, working part-time, directing a non-profit, and putting in lab hours for graduate school to sitting in my childhood bedroom thinking what was going through my 12-year-old mind to paint my walls such an atrocious purple. My whole life, I have had some schedule; I was always on the go, I always had something to do, and for the first time in my 22 years on the Earth, I had nothing to do, which drove me crazy. This period was like sitting in a waiting room, but for five months with absolutely nothing to do but nothing to think about except my new job in July, which may be the sunny patch of grass I could reach with just a little bit more walking.

HEALING

Being a first-year teacher during COVID-19 and starting online with my first class ever was kind of a sigh of relief. It wasn't just me who had no idea what was going on or what to do; it was a motif throughout the whole school of the unknown. I had an inner feeling: 'Well if I do mess up, at least other tenured teachers also have no idea how to work in this new educator world', since instructing through a Zoom camera was new to everyone. And I did so much messing up in my first year of teaching. I was teaching a subject I had no passion or background information for (Eureka math), was a pushover to all my scholars, and had no clue how to achieve the 'perfect classroom' that I was taught in Teach for America. Plus, with the social issues and the pandemic in the background of my classroom, I genuinely thought, 'Why?' How can my students care about fractions when they had shared with me family members dying due to COVID-19? How do you transition conversations with Black and Brown 9- and 10-year-olds from the Black Lives Matter\ protests happening in their backyards to how to divide two-digit numbers? So many times, during my first year, the lesson plans and the turn-and-talks fell into the background. If I had to pick a theme for my first year of teaching, it would be healing. Yes, we broke out the manipulatives, took quizzes and tests, and tried to get down some number sense. Still, at the end of the day, I had ninety human beings experiencing the broken outside world just like I was, and we had to talk and figure out how we would move on and progress together so that Eureka's scripted lesson plan didn't seem so important.

MOMENTS

The rest of my teaching career went by slowly but quickly. I finally got to teach a subject I had been passionate about ever since my mom dropped Toni Morrison's *The Bluest Eye* into my lap as a fourth grader, reading. I had kids that tested my nerves and were never absent, and I had kids that I will honestly never forget the impact they had on my life during this time. My school, co-workers, and scholars gave me something I had been searching for my whole life: a sense of a Black community. The beauty of teaching and learning with people who look like me gave me such a sense of self that I extended my teaching by a year; the two years didn't seem like enough, and I wasn't ready to leave my kids. Teaching is not about the time but the moments you share with your scholars. In these moments, you learn to twist and manipulate the standard curriculum to accommodate your unique and individualized students. In these moments, you learn the valuable lessons that secure the link in the chain that extends from the teacher to the scholars.

In my three years as a teacher, the most important lesson I learned is that a scholar is a person before they are a student. It sounds evident in a statement, but it was a hard lesson in practice. The role of a teacher is not limited to an academic outline or only exists within the hours of 8 am to 3 pm. The personal support and multiple factors that need to be considered when creating a foundation that a child can learn and build upon are vast and extend farther from their academic needs to their personal ones. Teaching my fourth-grade students, I realized that not only do I need to have a solid lesson plan that incorporates a balance between group critical thinking and individual mastery, but also, maybe the most important thing, is an extra hairbrush and edge gel. This is because when my students show up to class and their caretakers did not have time to comb their hair, they are more focused on their appearance than my lesson. I learned quickly that hair care, lotion, and deodorant were just as essential to have at the ready in my classroom as pencils and paper. The lesson plan or the amount of time I spent in preparation for the material doesn't matter; if a student walks into the classroom not wanting to learn, they won't. Nothing will be picture-perfect; just like teachers have off days, so do the students being taught.

OH, SO YOU 'BLACK' BLACK!

The first time I was asked if I was mixed race, I was in the first grade. It was by my first-grade teacher right outside of the hallway before recess. I was trying to make my light-up Sketchers work to impress my friends with my fast-as-lightning track skills and how my shoes added to my full Olympic ability. Mrs. Watson looked down at me and said, 'Carson, you're mixed, right?' She sounded so sure of herself and convinced of her assumption that I said, 'Yes'. She smiled, a smile of satisfaction in confirming her stereotypes and being assured that, yes, everything fits where it is supposed to in the world. Honestly, I had no idea what that term meant, and when I went home to ask my mom, she screamed at me about 'not letting anyone take away your own identity'. Being six years old, I did not see the big deal and just said, 'Yes, ma'am', to ensure I got a dessert that night after dinner. That was the first in a lifelong journey of defending my race to people close to me and strangers. I am not mixed; my parents are Black, and when I look in the mirror, I see a Black woman, but when I walk into the outside world, the perception of my identity is seen differently. And it always has been. There has been a sprinkle of ignorant comments since I can remember:

'Oh, you're lying; show me a picture of your family'.

'Are you sure you're not adopted?'

'But you talk white'.

'But you're pretty'.

'You don't even have the nose and lips of a Black girl'.

'Are you sure you're not Mexican?'

At my college's Black Students Association meeting, I was told I couldn't speak because I was a 'halfy'. Working in my school, two co-workers started a bet to see who was right about my race. Was I 'Black' Black or just mixed? Trying to find space in a community I had a birthright to be in became exhausting. I was always hyper-aware of my appearance when discussing race, especially when discussing such topics with Black people who did not know me. I was sure to come up with hard facts and research to secure my knowledge in the conversation to secure my Black card, which I felt I had to work hard to achieve. This was my whole life, being ready to defend my identity and place, speaking up in the all-White spaces I grew up in, and being prepared for any controversial topic that came my way. So, when George Floyd died, and everyone was ready to discuss race relations in the United States, I had nothing left to say.

I believe in communication and the power of words. I believe that one conversation could change my outlook on life, and I believe that the solution to a lot of the problems in the world is to talk with the desire for understanding. But how do I have conversations and communicate to people that, as a Black person, I have the right to live? At the very least, the conversations surrounding George Floyd's murder should have been justifications that a Black person has the right to exist and not be brutally murdered. Even that point was met with controversy, and I was tired and done. For the first time in a long time, I had no more energy to bring facts and research to the conversation. I had no more energy to put effort into my mantra that 'communication can change the world'. I had no more energy to justify to people how Black people deserve to take up space.

SO, WHAT NOW?

In 2023, I started my doctorate programme in clinical psychology and transitioned out of teaching. I did not expect to miss education so much, but I think about my previous school and scholars constantly. Even though I was a teacher for only three years, it is a part of me that will never entirely leave. When I think of how to use my degree and the process of getting my doctorate to create resources and knowledge of mental health for the Black community, I think of representation and access—creating spaces with other Black mental health professionals that generate education through conversation and connection. The mental health field has a reputation of being a gated community that only some people can break through; the first step in the process of creating this conversation in unseen communities is by breaking down the gates to foster equity. This is an enormous task, and currently, I do not have all the answers on how to accomplish this effectively. Still, I do think it starts with speaking up in spaces to give a voice to the underrepresented and generating research and work that furthers access to all, not just people who can get through the gate. I am only in the first year of my graduate programme, and through the people I have met in the field and the research I have been included in, the initial step in the process has already started. Throughout my time in the programme, it will only accelerate and push further towards the goal of representation and access. Working towards accomplishing this task, representing people who look like me, and taking up space in a field built upon excluding many minoritized communities, I remember to question everything and always speak up.

CHAPTER 6

A NEW RESPECT

Deidra Parker
Uplift Ascend Primary, USA

ABSTRACT

Holding the weight of the world can feel like an unimaginable burden. Black women educators' too often neglect their personal physical, emotional, and spiritual health and well-being due to familial and/or professional obligations. In this chapter, Deidra details her family's struggle with the stress of dual pandemics: COVID-19 and racial injustice in north Texas and beyond. Her story is grounded in a transparent desire to reframe the narrative around anxiety, addiction, and supportive communities.

Keywords: Emotional toll; stress and anxiety; work-life balance; support for teachers; technology in education; personal sacrifice

Figure 6.1 depicts what I am currently feeling as an educator—it shows a Black woman in a plastic bag screaming, maybe suffocating. I have those days often where I feel like I am suffocating. There is no escaping, and I am slowly dying inside, questioning myself if this is truly the job for me or worth losing my sanity. COVID-19 made me feel like I had nowhere to go and no one to turn to. I was crumbling inside because there was no 'fix' for it. Scared and grieving, I questioned myself about my career choice, but I refused to give up. Some days I am happy and content with my job as an educator and the work I do to close the gap for our children, while

Figure 6.1 Black and white image of woman screaming. From crumbling Black woman: A real-life tale, by S. Stewart-Bouley, 2023, https://blackgirlinmaine.com/health/crumbling-black-woman-a-real-life-tale/. Copyright 2023 by S. Stewart-Bouley.

other days I still question if I am still making a difference in someone's child life/education. I am sad teachers feel they must change their profession and seek a profession that will bring them peace and sanity because of unheard concerns. I feel overwhelmed at times—under-appreciated, overworked and underpaid as well—however, I have yet to determine if I will give up my profession because I feel undervalued. I teach because of children, specifically because of the impact my first-grade teacher made on my life. Although I have days where I struggle, I continue to teach because of my love of education and my desire to encourage children to embrace education that will lead to a better 'you', better life, and life experience.

COVID-19 was a life changing experience for us—more shifts in circumstances for some and more tragedy and grief for others. There were so many unanswered questions, speculations, jokes, assumptions, and blame for the virus. We, as a people, a nation, and the world, did not respect the virus. I do not feel that we gave it the focus and attention it deserved until multitudes of people started dying. COVID-19 did not care if we were young, old, healthy, rich, poor or had health issues—it ran amok, wild, and free among us without fear someone would find a way to cure it or slow it down. I feared the virus but that was not until later, after I started watching the news—seeing and hearing the toll it was taking on people's lives. The virus left me in tears, scared, and stressed. I found myself praying and grieving for those I did not know and those close to me.

When COVID-19 was first presented to us, I was in Louisiana for spring break visiting my family. I received an email from the school I was currently employed with stating we were not returning from spring break as scheduled because of the virus and we would receive more information regarding how and when we would be returning. Having to close school temporarily was new for everyone and no one was certain how to manage this situation. I was like, 'Hell yeah!' and I called my daughter to ask if she had read the email since we teach at the same school. My daughter was ecstatic that we were not returning to school and so was I because we were tired. We did not know the true meaning of tired, but we would find out. COVID-19 would teach us a lesson. We became students, and it became our teacher. Teaching was now done by trial and error, and life was no longer as it was. It was about not knowing who to trust and always wondering if those around you were trying to stay safe.

In the second week school was closed, we received notification we were going to teach virtually for a half day. 'What the hell?' I thought, 'How was that going to happen?' I had so many questions and thought this was going to be a disaster. How in the world did administration expect us to teach first grade scholars virtually when some of them could barely try to keep still in class? COVID-19 was about to take control of our classrooms. The plan was that we were each going to teach our own class until the end of school, until a better plan of action was drawn up for the following school year.

I had to go to school and pick up supplies I thought I would need for teaching my class—including a document camera and white board. We used Zoom to teach virtually; the scholars received hard copy work packets and had to upload it via Class Dojo for grading purposes. It was a hot mess, but what could we do? This experience was new for everyone. Some parents were able to upload their scholars' work via Class Dojo while others had no clue how to do it, so they sent me their work via my school email address. I had to grade what was submitted through Class Dojo and go look for parents' emails, which took a while because we were constantly receiving emails because of COVID-19. We had to constantly reach out to parents and communicate about any missing work, failing scholars, and check on their well-being. But who was checking on ours; was it family members; the school, friends? I felt my family did not truly understand my fear of this virus because they did not respect my ask of them to please do not be in crowds or amongst their friends who may have been around others and taking chances, playing Russian roulette with their lives. We met online via Zoom for meetings and our director (principal) did her best to check on everyone and allow them to talk about their situation; how they were holding out, holding on. You could see the anxiety of some; the calmness of others and the ones who were falling apart; the ones it was taking a toll on. I remember looking at a peer on camera, listening to her speaking and immediately texted my director and asked her if anyone had spoken to the peer about her welfare because I could see, hear she was not faring well.

I think the best thing about teaching virtually was rolling out of bed, brushing my teeth, putting on a school t-shirt, wearing slippers, and leaving on my pajama bottoms. I was professionally dressed from the top up, but my bottoms were very questionable at times. I had to put a sign on the door so no one would ring the doorbell to keep my dog from barking. My finger stayed ready to hit mute not only for myself but also for my scholars' parents. You just never knew what was going to be said or heard. My grandsons were in primary school at the same time we were teaching, and they both came over to my house for school because my daughter and I live across the street from each other.

My oldest grandson worked on his own while the youngest, who was in kindergarten, had to have someone help him. After school was out, my daughter would come over to my house. We became professional drinkers. It did not matter the time of day, the occasion, or if anyone said anything—we drank. Drinking became a daily habit and our means of dealing with the stress of the pandemic and teaching virtually. Every day, we laughed, cried, complained, and planned all over drinks. One day, the grocery store near us was going out of business, and we bought enough alcohol for approximately four to five people—but only two of us drank it. Hell, we each had a grocery cart full of alcohol. We had wine, beer, and wine coolers for days.

We drank so much one day, my daughter put her bottle cap over her eye like a pirate. I laughed, took a picture of her, and she fell asleep with her head on the table. I had to go to bed, and it was only 7 p.m. The next day, I decided we needed to slow down and stop drinking daily. We drank too much. We were dealing with COVID-19 in our own way, but we needed to find another means to deal with our worry besides alcohol. I did not want us to become alcoholics because it was getting easier and easier by the day to drink daily. We survived the rest of the school year, but what would the next school term bring? At the end of the school year, we had to pack up our classrooms. It felt completely weird going into a classroom I had left as expecting to return—it was as if time had stood still in that classroom. I felt sad and melancholy about the end of our school year, stressed about the next school year and the increased learning gap for our scholars. While facing challenges teaching virtually, I had my own personal issues I was dealing with as well.

Wearing a mask in public or anywhere was new for us, for me especially. The mask was hot and made me break out. I have sensitive skin and wearing a mask was terrible but necessary. I stayed home and did not venture out much. The only place I went to was to the grocery store, and I was reluctant to do that. Whenever someone was in line behind me and coughed or sneezed, I did like some of us did—I turned and looked at them and moved up a few steps. I can laugh at that now but not then. I was scared. I hate I felt that way—the need to move. I was scared I would contract COVID-19 though, bring it home to my mom, and she would die because of me. My mom has health issues, such as diabetes, high blood pressure, high cholesterol and breast and kidney cancer. I did not want to be the one to cause my mom any harm.

I was scared of everyone, and I found myself praying for those I knew and those I did not know because I was watching too many news broadcasts. I was carrying the weight of the world on my shoulders and grieving daily. My adult children, on the other hand, were out and about around their friends, going to public places without masks. In Texas, you had a choice when COVID-19 was broadcasted—you could choose to wear a mask or go without it. The bars were open and in full effect without any measures or precautions in place; there was nothing in restaurants protecting people from one another. My children thought they would not, or could not, get COVID-19. We had several conversations about it with them all ending with I was taking it too seriously and stressing too much. My son went out with friends to his local hangout only to find out a couple of days after going that his favourite bartender and server had contracted COVID-19.

He, along with his other two friends, had to take the test and wait for their results. I told my son he could not come to my house, to stay away, and do not immediately come over if his results were negative because I wanted to give it some time, just in case he started feeling bad later. He thought I was joking, called me one day and said he was coming over. I told him, 'Oh hell no! Stay where you are at'. It hurt my heart to tell him to stay home, but he needed to know I was serious. He stayed away for more than ten days. He said that was the hardest thing he has ever done in his life—staying away from me.

My oldest daughter, like my son, was hanging out with friends; going to choir rehearsal and was just everywhere. Unfortunately, she, unlike my son, caught COVID-19, not once but twice. It scared the life out of me when she got it the first time. I prayed that she would survive. I cried every time I thought of her and the possibility of her outcome. I brought her food and medicine wearing a mask, sprayed Lysol or Microban in front of her door, dropped it off and called her once I left so we would not have any contact. The second time my daughter had COVID-19 was worse than her first time. She was having problems breathing, and the coughing and shortness of breath was terrible. I thought I was scared the first time, but her second bout with COVID-19 almost gave me a nervous breakdown.

I called her all day, asked ten million questions, and probably got on her nerves. When she got COVID-19 a second time, I decided to get the vaccine. My original plan was to wait a year, see the outcome, and then get it according to the results and side effects of others. I told my children of my decision to get the vaccine and my oldest said something crazy. She said I would have side effects from the shot that were going to be detrimental and turn into a zombie. I immediately thought, 'Whose child is this? Surely, she does not belong to me! Turn into a zombie!' If she did not look so much like me, I would have thought I was given the wrong child at birth. It made me question what the world were my child's beliefs and who exactly was she hanging out with and the conversations they were having. My sister had to be rushed to the hospital and had to be put on oxygen because COVID-19 had attacked her and become a part of her life. I thought, 'Here we go again'. The waiting game—waiting to see if she survived.

In August 2020, summer vacation had come and gone just like that with the company of face masks and nowhere to go but home; it was time for the new school term, stress and the unknown. Prior to school starting, it was decided we would offer parents various means of schooling for their scholars. They too, like us, were working from home. While some had gone back, the majority were still working from home. Parents were given the choice of having their scholars taught virtually, hybrid (scholars learn virtually a couple of days and come in person for a few days), or in person. The teachers, on the other hand, had to report in person unless there was a health issue. I was anxious about which form of teaching I would have to do, and I can remember thinking, 'Lord, please do not let it be virtual. I have had my fill of virtual'.

Well, guess what it was: virtual. We had to use Zoom and another application while teaching virtually and had to use one inside of the other. I will always remember the day we had training; it was the only time I cried during and after training. I was so lost during training, and I thought, 'How am going to teach my scholars when I do not know what I am doing?' I was stressed beyond belief. I had to have a self-talk and convince myself I could teach virtually—yeah right.

I had no confidence in myself and felt I would fail my scholars. I wrote down what I could remember from the training and practiced until I felt comfortable. On top of writing and submitting lesson plans, making a webpage for each subject I taught, I was now required to grade the scholars work online; submit homework and copies of it; include a class/parent newsletter; teach live. Everything was done via those applications. The virtual class I taught was so big (with 40 scholars). I had a morning and afternoon class. It was very stressful, and I went back to drinking. I think I spent more at the liquor store than the grocery store. Administration wanted us to add a Bitmoji of ourselves on our homepage. 'Well', I thought, 'unless someone is going to do that for me, they better feel my welcome via my words!' Nope, I did not do it. That was too much stress for someone trying to keep their head above water and keep from drowning.

I eventually became more comfortable with entering the information and teaching online, but then I had issues with my scholars and their parents at times. Some of it was hilarious, and some of it got on my damn nerves. Parents were completing their scholar's homework. Some did not even bother to allow the scholars to copy what they had written; they turned in the homework in their handwriting. I did not grade the work but gave them three opportunities to correct the handwriting before grading it. The parents were also helping with their diagnostic assessments. According to their scores, the scholars were geniuses. The majority were in first grade but on a fourth-grade level. Now, I'm not saying that cannot happen, but most of them? The parents thought by giving their scholar the answer they were helping him/her, which is not true. It was not a true assessment of what the scholars knew.

The second time we had to give the test the scholars had to come in person. The parents, scholars, and I were all scared. COVID-19 was still running amok among us. One little girl was so scared I had to sit her next to me. She looked like she was ready to run out, cry, and faint all at once. I knew her fear though. The parents complained if little Susie or Tom received a failing grade, but I think it was because the parents had failed the first-grade work. A parent blamed me for her scholar failing because I had not contacted her about it. I had, but she never answered so I called her husband. I had spoken with the dad at least three times, and he said he would get with the grandmother because he was the one helping the scholar.

Mom was not too happy with my information because dad had not addressed the issue. It was never addressed, and he was one of those that never turned in any work. It was frustrating to see the educational gap widening. I was irate that some parents did nothing; some did the bare minimum; and few truly did help. While I understood they had to work, this was their child's education. I saw and heard a little of everything and was always mute ready. One parent walked behind his scholar's camera every morning with his T-shirt and boxers on. Another parent had on a T-shirt and jeans and needed a shirt. He elbowed crawled on his belly on the floor behind his scholar, stuck his hand into the drawer for his shirt, and smiled. I did not have the heart to tell him I had seen him because he was so proud of himself. He thought no one had seen him; I laughed so hard.

One of my scholars was in his bed with his scooter trying to ride it in bed. There were sleeping scholars, as well as scholars who took pictures of themselves and put them on the screen so I would think they were in class. I heard one parent tell her child he, 'better behave and pay attention, or I'll beat your behind!' Yes, I was always mute ready. A scholar asked permission to go to the bathroom; however, when I checked to see if he had returned, he had placed his dog in his seat. Priceless! It was moments like that that made my heart glad. I learned so much more about my scholars in that year than I normally do in my in-person classroom. I was introduced to younger and older siblings, dolls and their names, chickens, pigs, ducks, and cats. I was given a tour of bedrooms or the room where they were learning.

The scholars were suffering socially but I, too, was suffering, I did not interact with any of my friends face to face. I had a parent to protect. Recognizing they were socially suffering, I decided to leave my students' microphones on during our 'recess' time and allow them to talk, look at television together, or whatever they wanted to do. I did not take my break so I could allow them that small amount of time together even if it was through a computer screen. Along with feeling sad, overwhelmed, and my heartbreaking, I was frustrated, as well with the peers I worked with. I was frustrated because I had been working hard to keep myself free of COVID-19 for my mom, family and now for my scholars' sakes. When we went back to school in person, I had to be tested twice within a two-week period. The first time I was like okay, 'I got this', but the second time, I lost my mind and broke down. With COVID-19 still kicking our butts, how in the hell were people without thought and restraint for others. This virus had us by the throat and was not letting go; I sank a little deeper into depression, and my drinking increased.

After our Christmas break, the parents were given the choice again to choose how their scholars would learn. I became a virtual and hybrid teacher because more parents chose in person learning. I was not only teaching online but also those that were in my classroom. I had a headache just about every day because it was very stressful teaching children virtually while teaching children in the classroom at the same exact time; I had to check the scholar's work online while actively monitoring scholar's work in the classroom. Do not get me wrong. I love my scholars, and I love what I do, but 2020–2021 was one hell of a year. It was a year full of emotions that took a toll on me. My mind and body were tired, but I was ready to do my job for my extended family (peers and administration) and scholars. Although I was ready to do what was required of me, I understand why some quit the teaching profession. They probably felt underappreciated, overworked without adequate pay, tired of dealing with the bull. No one gave back to them; they were depressed, tired, and questioned if this was something they could work through for the rest of their work lives. Was work worth their sanity or their happiness? Sometimes, we still wonder. Teaching for me means more than just a job. It is a means of helping others and that is something I always want to do in my life—help others in way I possibly can. Who better to help than our babies? Hopefully, I make an impact in someone's life like my first-grade teacher did in mine. While COVID-19 kept its ugly and demanding self in the news, there were three words the world came together on, agreed upon and fought over, 'I can't breathe'.

I do not know where I was or what I was doing when I heard those words, 'I can't breathe'. I do know it was gut wrenching, heartbreaking, brought me to my knees and had me crying. As I write this, I still find it hard to discuss without crying. I did not know George Floyd, but it grieves me to think a grown man had to call out to his mom for help as he might have had when he was a little boy. It angers me to know that things like this can still happen in this nation at this point in time. If this had happened when the KKK was more prominent in 1885 and were running amok with their hatred in the backwoods, when Black people had to sit in the back of the bus, separate entry ways, and separate water fountains, it would be a little more understandable, ugly, but understandable. Have we really evolved as a nation, as a world, as people, in some respects, yes. I believe that we still have room for growth though. I think some have learned from past mistakes, but there is still plenty of hatred that has just been swept under the rug. I saw the hatred of others when I was a little girl, when my family was made to enter the doctor's office by the back door; that hatred still exists today but comes in different faces, actions, and wears a different costume.

It angered me that a Black man (police officer) stood there, watched, and did nothing to help another Black man. It angered me that men stood there and did nothing to help—another human being. I was furious that men thought they were above the law, that the hatred I witnessed as a child was going to be seen by the babies of today and the future of tomorrow. When will there truly be justice, equality for all? When will we truly learn to respect our differences and not fear the differences but learn from each other? One group protested the wrong of George Floyd while the others mocked their words. I did not make signs or protest regarding the 'Black Lives Matter' slogan because Black people lives have always mattered to me. Everyone's life has always mattered to me regardless of their colour.

One would think all people's lives matter to the human race; however, the slogan was taken out of context and words of war evolved, ugly words, words that showed people's true selves. I questioned why someone's life still did not matter today. What does matter to them, if not a human life? I was angry, hurt, and disappointed that Mr Floyd's life did not appear to matter to those that had taken an oath to protect him. What matters to me is the racial injustice people of colour still must endure and the outcome. What matters is the fear one still has embedded in his/her heart because of racial injustice. What matters is when are we truly going to be free? What mattered was George Floyd.

COVID-19 taught me lessons that year. I learned I am much stronger than I ever thought I was because it took a heart of love and steel to push forward during COVID-19 not only in my personal life but also my professional life. I wanted to quit and give up a lot of days but knew I would not. The scholars, their parents, my peers, and my family depended on me. I also learned, let's not say learned but was reminded, how ugly people can be because one is different and still fear the unknown about people. Their hate was swept under the rug and was retrieved all in the blink of an eye. I was also reminded how easy it is to become an alcoholic, but learned life choices are not easy, and one must choose the right path to take, or their life will be drastically altered. I chose the path that will forever lead me to advocate for children, for people—to keep fighting to close the learning gap for our children.

REFERENCE

Stewart-Bouley, 2023 Stewart-Bouley, S. (2023). Crumbling Black woman: A real life tale [Photograph]. *Black Girl in Maine Media*. https://blackgirlinmaine.com/health/crumbling-black-woman-a-real-life-tale/

CHAPTER 7

ROCK STEADY: AN AUTOETHNOGRAPHY EXPLORING MY LIVED EXPERIENCES DURING DUAL PANDEMICS

Meghan L. Green
Erikson Institute, USA

ABSTRACT

Black women are often asked to splinter themselves into small, easily digestible piece that fit neatly into boxes. They should either be logical, rational purveyors of knowledge or hyper-empathetic caregivers. Utilizing autoethnography and poetic inquiry, Meghan's story offers a both/and perspective rooted in endarkened feminist onto-epistemological understandings of how Black women's lives defy tightly prescribed binaries. She reflects on the tension between self-care and communal care in hopes of sitting somewhere in the center.

Keywords: Poetic inquiry; communal care; educator well-being; identity affirmation; liberatory education; collective responsibility

INTRODUCTION

I am a Black queer cisgender woman who was raised between two small, rural towns in southwest Louisiana surrounded by soybean fields and dusty back roads. My mom was a high school English teacher who routinely took on multiple jobs to make ends meet and to fund me and my younger brother's wild aspirations. When I was about 11 years old, I remember hearing Tupac Shakur's (1995) 'Dear Mama' for the first time – 'And when it seems that I'm hopeless/You say the words that can get me back in focus'. Those lyrics felt complicated to me at the time because, like Tupac, I had a convoluted relationship with my mother. As a budding teenager, I often fought against the lessons she tried to teach me. Her words felt full of judgement, and I could not accept their meaning at face value. She had grown up between two periods of unrest – Jim Crow segregation and the Civil Rights era integration. Her worldview had been shaped by the juxtaposition of her youth and subsequent experiences as a wife and mother. Her words felt heavy and often reminded me of the burdens placed on Black women to carry generations of hopes and dreams while tucking our own somewhere neatly to the side.

Her words also held a special kind of power that could manifest such amazing strength in me. I can only imagine the resolve she mustered as she whispered them to her ancestors during her nightly prayers. Those words inspired me to follow in her footsteps when choosing my career. Eventually, I became an educator because I was drawn to young children's curiosity and firmly believed that I was called to channel my passion for inquiry into this profession. I taught pre-kindergarten to 4th grade for over 15 years in Texas and Louisiana. As I reflected on my mother's words over the years, my pedagogy shifted to include a more direct utilization of anti-bias and anti-racist ideals that held space for humanizing early learning settings for all children. The following autoethnography chronicles my personal and professional experiences as an early childhood educator in north Texas from 2020 to 2022. Each piece of my story includes a poetic offering that seeks to '…capture rhythm and holistic voice…' (Cutts & Waters, 2019, p. 7) and provide the reader with a grounded sensory experience.

LIFE NOTES FROM THE MARGINS OF THE MYTHICAL NORM

'Mahogany: A haiku for strength and steadfast resolve'

The scar has three lines:
One for her father, her son,
And her living ghost. (Green, 2021, Original poem)

In November 2014, my car flipped over three times on a slick highway not too far from my friend's apartment. I walked away from this traumatic ordeal with only a few scrapes and scratches. The above poem represents both the literal scars that can still be seen on my right hand and the figurative scars that have adorned me for the last 39 years. The first line on my scar is for my father. I am a spitting image of my dad. He was born in 1961 and is an inspired son of Parliament Funkadelic, Afrofuturist musical pioneers (Peattie, 2022). Coming of age in the 1970s and 80s, his inquisitive spirit and restless nature drove his ambition and will to persevere as a young man. He and my mother divorced when I was 7 years old, and I spent most of my childhood and adolescence chasing his shadow. My paternal extended family, including my grandmother, my grandfather, my uncles, and a host of aunts and cousins, watched over my brother and I in his absence. They made sure that I understood my father's tortured genius as a little Black girl moving through the world looking for a certain tenderness and care. Eventually, our paths crossed again, and our complementary spirits reconciled. My dad's capricious period had ended, and he had developed a cool and calm demeanor that made him the perfect listening ear when things just seemed to fall apart.

The second line of my scar is for my oldest son, Zion Amir. He was born prematurely at 23 weeks due to an undiagnosed infertility issue. He died only 1 hour after he took his first breath. I was 23 years old when I lost my child. Over the years, I have often reflected on the impact that his death had on my life. I had only been teaching pre-kindergarten for one year before he died. I remember having dreams about what he would be like when he was a toddler. What would his first words be? How could I ensure that he never searched for validation outside of himself like I had done for so many years? How could I ensure that he felt loved beyond a shadow of a doubt in a world that saw his very existence as a Black boy as threatening? Two years after Zion's death, I gave birth to my son, Terry and then later my son, Camren. It seemed that the universe was intent on providing me the chance to raise children who embodied self-confidence and pride in themselves and their heritage. I began my graduate studies in early childhood education when my sons were young. They were the vessels that held my hopes and dreams for creating classroom environments that honored children from historically marginalized backgrounds. Environments that fostered what Doucet (2017) referred to as a 'community of trust' where children and families thrived in authenticity.

The third scar on my hand is for what I refer to as my living ghost. It is the specter that haunts me regardless of how brightly the sun is shining. My journey with mental health, specifically bi-polar disorder, has taken me on a multitude of twists and turns. It first manifested while I was a junior at Howard University. I entered the university as a Laureate scholar on a full ride scholarship due to my high academic achievement in high school. I had always been driven to succeed beyond anyone's expectations of me. I routinely outperformed my counterparts while struggling to silence the little voice of doubt inside of me. Doubt that caused me to question my abilities and talents as well as my worthiness to receive the accolades I earned. This self-doubt is a common thread in the literature about Black women scholars who occupy white heteronormative spaces (Wingfield, 2015). One day during my junior year, I decided to stop attending my classes. I fell into a deep depression while continuing to perform being good enough. Several of my close friends called my mother, and she recommended that I seek out a therapist at the university counseling center. I only attended a few therapy sessions that semester, but I learned a great deal about the ghost who haunted me for most of my childhood and adolescence. It would be another decade before I was officially diagnosed with bi-polar disorder.

My living ghost reminds me of the pressures Black women face because of both our gendered and racialized lived experiences. A myriad of factors influence how we bring ourselves into educational settings as educators. The three diminutive scars on my right hand serve as remembrances of the lived experiences that have shaped my pedagogical development and tested my resolve as an early childhood educator. I could not have imagined how extensive this test would be as I entered the 2019–2020 school year.

COVID-19 PANDEMIC AND TEACHING

'Invisible Woman'

Hiding behind the mask of resilience,
she occupies a space reserved for those whose strength
is often the subject of pop culture references.
Independence
Grit
Resolve
These become synonyms well-meaning folks use
when they forget her name and just call her
Mule. (Green, 2023c, p. 90)

Be bold. Be brave. Be you. I can remember walking into the store and seeing the words printed on this dainty little 7 × 7-inch canvas framed in a stylized floral arrangement accented with hues of grey, pink, and green (see Figure 7.1). The words seemed to call out to me like the lyrics of one of my favorite songs. Prompting me to remember that I possessed the necessary strength to face challenges I could only imagine. Spring of 2020 brought those challenges right to my front door when my principal informed me that we would not be returning to school after the break due to the

Figure 7.1 Canvas print with flowers and my mantra. Photo credit, Meghan L. Green.

imminent threat of the COVID-19 outbreak. This decision was announced amid a divided political climate where the health of students and teachers became a debate topic for conservative and liberal politicians alike.

For the first time in recent history, all pre-kindergarten to 12th grade schools were mandated to operate virtually while offering asynchronous and synchronous lessons for students. My second-grade team's group chat was flooded with concerns from my colleagues about how exactly asynchronous learning would function with seven- and eight-year-old children. During our campus leadership meeting, I carefully listened to my principal explain the district's guidelines and our campus' expectations for teachers. The district created work packets in math and reading and mailed them to students' homes. My team and I frantically contacted parents through email and phone calls attempting to answer as many questions as we could. Unfortunately, there were days when we just did not have the answers. Our days were spent trying to soothe our students, their families, and each other.

Amid this uncertainty, I had to admit an uncomfortable truth. Some part of me was relieved to have some extra time away from the daily demands of teaching. In addition to being a single mother and an early childhood educator, I was a fifth-year doctoral student who was knee-deep in my final doctoral courses making my way toward my dissertation proposal. Selfishly, a part of me was already laying the guidelines for a new and improved writing schedule that would maximize my productivity. I began devoting time that should have been dedicated to rest and a renewed focus on my health to routines that further entrenched me in what Tricia Hersey (2022) referred to as grind culture. From March 2020 to October 2020, I followed a meticulous schedule on every weekday: (1) waking up at 4:00 a.m. to write or revise portions of my dissertation proposal; (2) then transitioning into my role as mama at 6:30 a.m. and getting Terry and Camren ready for virtual classes; and (3) finally switching to teacher mode and preparing to engage 18 third-grade students on Zoom from 8:00 a.m. to 12:00 p.m. and attending professional development/leadership meetings in the afternoons from 1:00 p.m. 3:00 p.m. I followed this delicate balance for months while my district concocted a plan for returning to school for a combination of in person, virtual, and hybrid instruction in the fall of 2020.

In October 2020, campus leaders met to review the plan for moving into a brand-new building. As grade level chair, I was designated the hybrid teacher of record. This meant that I had one section of third graders who would attend school in person Monday through Friday; one section who would attend in person on Mondays and Tuesdays and virtually Wednesday through Friday; and one section who would attend virtually Monday through Wednesday and in person on Thursdays and Fridays. This hybrid schedule was difficult to manage at first. We managed so many technical difficulties as students were often at home with caregivers who were trying to balance their own virtual work schedules and troubleshoot new learning platforms with multiple young children. Those first few months back in person also presented new challenges. Students had not been in a physical school building since March 2020. Following social distancing guidelines, we were relegated to our classrooms for most of the day. Staff delivered breakfast and lunch to our rooms each day and outdoor recess was nonexistent. From 7:10 a.m. to 3:00 p.m., my students and I struggled to adjust to this new normal.

My sons attended school in person during this time because of my teaching obligations. They had also just transferred from the suburban school district we lived in into the charter school network in which I taught. This transition ended up being one of the most impactful decisions I had ever made as a parent because of the positive influence my colleagues had on my sons. Most of my sons' previous teachers had been White women. Over eighty percent of the teachers on my campus were Black or Latinx. Terry and Camren were finally surrounded with educators who shared their racial and ethnic identities. I believe that my colleagues demonstrated a higher level of care and concern for my children because of their shared identities.

The literature on Black women educators demonstrates that educators who employ culturally relevant pedagogy must ensure that their beliefs about teaching align with their instructional practices (Gardner et al., 2020). Like the connection between academic knowledge and lived experiences found in Black feminist thought, culturally relevant educators are identified as such by both their beliefs and actions (Beauboeuf-Lafontant, 1997; Green, 2023b; Hodge, 2017; Ladson-Billings, 2002). In culturally relevant classrooms, educators measure success through lenses other than those imposed by the White dominant culture (Ladson-Billings, 2002; Ware, 2006). Black women teachers who employ culturally relevant pedagogy advocate for the critique of academic measures that assess students' familiarity of dominant norms more than anything else.

My colleagues provided my sons with learning spaces that honored who they were as Black boys. This made all the difference for my family and I during this chaotic time. The 2020–2021 school year was filled with a combination of painful trials and triumphant occurrences. I firmly believe that we all survived this period because of the communal care in which we grounded the space. That year taught us the value of leaning on one another and trusting an enigmatic process. We did not know how much that trust would mean in the coming months as we witnessed the world around us catch fire.

RACIAL JUSTICE IN TEXAS

'Horror Noire/Banned Books'

Our horror stories are tales
We pass down to our children.
They call it history;
We call it memories.
This is why anti-racism is the only option.
We hold the scars of our ancestors.
They speak into us and
Into our victory against the things that go bump in night.
Our vampires walk proudly in the sunlight chanting,
'Make America Great Again!' (Green, 2023, Original poem)

Sometimes I sit and replay his final words repeatedly – I can't breathe. George Floyd reminded me of my father and my uncles. The stories his eyes told did not seem to match his final words. As he struggled for air and looked for help from those around him, I imagined the terror he felt. I thought about my sons who were quickly growing taller than me at nine and ten years old and about the frightening encounters I have had with police officers in the District of Columbia, Texas, and Louisiana. As I replayed these thoughts, I fought back the same tears of anger and anguish that flooded my eyes when reading stories about Trayvon Martin, Tamir Rice, Sandra Bland, Michael Brown, Botham Jean, and Breonna Taylor. One name stung a bit more, however, because of her immediate proximity – Atatiana Jefferson. Atatiana was only 28 years old when she was murdered in her home by a White police officer in Fort Worth, Texas. She earned her bachelor's degree from Xavier University in New Orleans and was a pre-medical graduate student (Killough & Levenson, 2022). Fort Worth had been my home for over two years, and I mourned the loss of yet another Black woman at the hands of law enforcement. These feelings pooled together, and in the summer of 2020, they spilled over into a call for action.

After processing my feelings and reflecting on decades of experiences and stories, I understood that the oppression of Black people in this country was not subsidized by one political party. Historically, both the Democratic and Republican parties have enacted legislation that harmed Black communities disproportionately. There was a general fear of an uprising against oppression in this country. Black peoples' screams of 'WE ARE HUMANS!' continued to fall on deaf ears. The Black Lives Matter movement reflected the post-super predator generational angst. We continued to fight for the acknowledgement of our humanity by people who sought to dehumanize us as a means of making themselves feel better about their despicable acts. My feelings about the oppression of racialized groups were amplified by the bigotry I saw promulgated across social media. I read the vitriol filled words of my peers, and my anger morphed into resolve. A resolve to change the status quo by unplugging from the anonymous void of cleaver handles and avatars and creating a new system that promoted the liberation of racialized groups through education. That education had to start in my home, with my sons.

My partner and I decided to take Terry and Camren to a Black Lives Matter protest in Oklahoma City in June 2020. Before attending the protest, we sat down with the boys and asked them to share what they knew about the recent events regarding racial injustice. We discussed the historical context of protests in the United States and shared details about our experiences with community organizing. I reminded the boys of the anti-White supremacy protest they attended in 2017 when they were 7 and 5 years old. I showed them pictures of the protest signs they hand painted and the slogans they wrote with crayons and markers. I also told them about the backlash our family received from some people on social media when I posted pictures of their earliest revolutionary moments. We wanted to be as transparent as possible about the state of things and to provide space for Terry and Camren to reflect on their feelings and thoughts about attending the event.

After we completed this initial discussion, we finalized our preparations for the protest and march. We packed food and water for ourselves and our comrades. We let our families know what our plans were just in case they needed to get in contact with us or us with them. We drove down to the rally site and made our way down the street noticing other families along the way. We were not the only parents who had decided that this summer was the time for our children to witness how anger, frustration, and sadness morphed into resolve, mutual aid, and community action. We spent hours marching from one rally to another as we made our way to the Oklahoma City Police Department. By the end of the day, we were tired, and the boys questioned why we had spent so much time engaging in something that they were still struggling to completely understand. We explained that our one day of protest was a small part of a larger movement. A movement that examined the logic behind carceral regimes and centered community care over punitive actions. Their wonderings led me to consider how other children were processing the world around them.

Later that summer, I called my principal to discuss the rumors my colleagues and I heard swirling around about plans to return safely to school in the fall. We worried about the district's commitment to everyone's safety. How would they prioritize the well-being of children and adults? Would that priority include our social and emotional selves? How were the administrators at the central office downtown demonstrating an authentic concern for racial injustice, specifically the anti-Black racism being exhibited all around us? These uncertainties loomed over our heads as we prepared to return to our essential positions as educators. I thought about the boys' questions after attending the protest in Oklahoma, and I asked my principal if I could create a space during the day for students to learn about and reflect on social justice issues. She approved my request, and I began writing weekly lesson plans focused on different topics related to race, ethnicity, language, gender, dis/ability, and class. Each lesson included a provocation meant to stimulate children's curiosity and activate their prior knowledge. I wanted to build a bridge between the Tik Tok reels my students were referencing throughout the day and the living history they were a part of.

With every pledge of commitment to anti-racism, there was an equally visceral reaction from people who wanted to preserve White supremacy culture. Those dominant narratives shifted from calls to unite the right to cries against a woke leftist agenda. Being home and socially isolated for months at the height of COVID-19 meant spending far more time scrolling through social media feeds attempting to keep up with the latest news. My students witnessed that shift firsthand and eagerly discussed what it meant for their generation. They wanted to know why they had never learned about certain events in history from diverse perspectives and why there were people in our community who did not honor everyone's humanity. Those questions were harder to answer, but over the course of the 2020–2021 school year I facilitated a learning environment that held space for the messy task of truth telling (Green, 2023a). Between trying to care for two young Black boys, completing a doctoral program, and trying to be an educator that would make my sons proud, I reflected on how I chose to move in a system sometimes inundated with performative allyship. We must actively dismantle racist systems in ways that go beyond sitting in trainings and talking about doing it. My current goal as an early childhood teacher educator is to disrupt deficit-oriented perspectives and support pre-service teachers as we collaborate and (re)imagine liberatory spaces for all children across intersections of identity.

LESSONS LEARNED FROM 2020–2022

'Ode to (In)Visible Struggles'

We smile to hide deep scars
Placed on hearts worn on our sleeves.
Scars that have scabbed over
And healed from the outside looking in.

They never heal though…not really.

They continue to fester behind those smiles
Bright enough to light up any room.
Smiles that have cracked at the corners
And created more doubt than comfort.

They never bring comfort though…not really.

They provide a testimony for those
Who witnessed each slow death.
Deaths that seem surprising
And cause onlookers to question.

They never ask the right questions though…not really. (Green, 2023, Original poem)

I learned the importance of care and well-being from teaching during the pandemic and the most recent heightened period of racial injustice. My most significant lesson centered on the interconnected nature of educator well-being. On the micro-level, I felt a renewed commitment to my personal well-being. As I navigated the pressures of motherhood, interpersonal relationships, early childhood education, and graduate school, I began to notice how little intentional time I spent on taking care of my heart and mind. There were times when I ignored my emotions to push through and get things done. In those times, I often felt the consequences through spirals with my mental health. Eventually, I recognized how unsustainable my behavior was and I shifted how I prioritized my well-being. Instead of putting myself last, I decided to honor my feelings first and curate spaces of joy, affirmation, and rest. This is a cyclical process for me that embodies the fluidity of my worldview. If I am not well, then I cannot reasonably nurture those around me.

My interpersonal relationships with my loved ones, including personal and professional connections, represent my meso-level of well-being. After I earned my doctorate in 2022, I transitioned out of the early childhood classroom and into teacher education. My sons and I moved from Texas to Illinois once I received my first postdoctoral job offer. This was a difficult transition away from our family and friends, but our new community welcomed us with open arms. We have been able to cultivate new, loving bonds that support our individual and collective well-being. My friends and colleagues in our new city provide caring spaces and listening ears. We have all been through so much over the last several years, and I have observed a purposeful move toward a communal ethic of care (Green, 2023b) that holds room for individuals and the community. This care extends into my relationships with my students in higher education as well. I strive to create a learning environment for preservice teachers that respects their lived experiences and centers transparency in the hopes that they will then implement these practices with young children and families. My focus on individual and communal care reflects my belief in the importance of dismantling binaries that insist that we must choose one over the other.

On the macro-level, early childhood educators' well-being has rarely been a topic of discussion (Bromer et al., 2023; Souto-Manning & Melvin, 2022). Early childhood educators were the backbone of care during the pandemic. Resilience was a word often used to describe educators who shouldered the burden of entering spaces where we cared for the children of others while silencing the nagging feeling that we were neglecting our own. Resilience has been weaponized against women educators of color, in particular, to justify our inequitable treatment in workplaces (Souto-Manning & Melvin, 2022). I have learned that, in some cases, resiliency can be understood as taking on the impossible while simultaneously making the impossible happen for other people. As I sat with this new narrative of resiliency, I pondered what this might mean for early childhood educators moving forward. How do early childhood educators explore the vastness of ourselves during times of uncertainty and upheaval? How have educators explored the vastness of what it means to lean in on each other inside and outside of turbulent times? As a community, early childhood educators experienced so much loss throughout the pandemic. That loss, however, made room for growth. When I think about well-being on a macro-level, I envision opportunities for us to grieve what we no longer have while dreaming of and creating the spaces that we only felt were unimaginable.

REFERENCES

Beauboeuf-Lafontant, T. (1997). *I teach you the way i see us: Concepts of self and teaching of African American women teachers committed to social justice.* https://files.eric.ed.gov/fulltext/ED408395.pdf

Bromer, J., Turner, C., Melvin, S., & Ray, A. (2023). "We are that resilience": Building cultural capital through family child care. *Contemporary Issues in Early Childhood, 25*(2), 202–222.

Cutts, Q. M., & Waters, M. B. S. (2019). Poetic approaches to qualitative data analysis. In *Oxford research encyclopedia of education*.

Doucet, F. (2017). What does a culturally sustaining learning climate look like? *Theory into Practice: Racial Disproportionality in Special Education: When Beliefs, Policies, and Practices Collide in the Pursuit of Equity, 56*(3), 195–204. https://doi.org/10.1080/00405841.2017.1354618

Gardner, R. P., Osorio, S. L., Carrillo, S., & Gilmore, R. (2020). (Re)membering in the pedagogical work of black and brown teachers: Reclaiming stories as culturally sustaining practice. *Urban Education, 55*(6), 838–864. https://doi.org/10.1177/0042085919892036

Green, M. (2023a). #Virtually_woke: Using digital media to support young children's development of critical consciousness. *Exchange*, (270), p. 63–66.

Green, M. L. (2023b). Building culturally situated relationships with BIPOC children through a communal ethic of care. *Early Childhood Education Journal, 52*(5), 935–948.

Green, M. L. (2023c). Invisible woman. In H. Van Rooyen, R. D'Abdon, A. Hough, D. Ndlovu, K. Pithouse-Morgan, M. Pete, B. Prince, & Y. Sliep (Eds.), *Voices unbound: Poems of the eighth international symposium on poetic inquiry* (p. 90). African Sun Press.

Hersey, T. (2022). *Rest is resistance: A manifesto*. Little, Brown Spark.

Hodge, R. Y. (2017). *Teaching is a revolutionary act: The legitimate knowledges of Black women teachers enacting activist literacies* (Publication No. 10272634) Doctoral dissertation. Syracuse University. ProQuest Dissertations and Theses.

Killough, A., & Levenson, E. (2022, December 12). Former officer who killed Atatiana Jefferson testifies she pointed a gun at him before he fired. *CNN.* https://www.cnn.com/2022/12/12/us/atatania-jefferson-aaron-dean-trial/index.html

Ladson-Billings, G. (2002). I ain't writin; nuttin': Permissions to fail and demands to succeed in urban classrooms. In L. Delpit & J. Dowdy (Eds.), *The skin that we speak: Thoughts on language and culture in the classroom* (pp. 107–120). New Press.

Peattie, P. (2022). Afrofuturism revelation and revolution; Voices of the digital generation. *Journal of Communication Inquiry, 46*(2), 161–184.

Shakur, T. (1995). Dear mama [Song]. On *Me against the world* [Album]. Interscope.

Souto-Manning, M., & Melvin, S. A. (2022). Early childhood teachers of color in New York City: Heightened stress, lower quality of life, declining health, and compromised sleep amidst COVID-19. *Early childhood research quarterly, 60*, 34–48.

Ware, F. (2006). Warm demander pedagogy: Culturally responsive teaching that supports a culture of achievement for African American students. *Urban Education, 41*(4), 427–456. https://doi.org/10.1177/0042085906289710

Wingfield, T. T. (2015). (Her) story: The evolution of a dual identity as an emerging Black female and scholar. In V. E. Evans-Winters & B. Love (Eds.), *Black feminism in education* (pp. 81–92). Peter Lang.

ADDITIONAL READING

Bass, L. (2012). When care trumps justice: The operationalization of Black feminist caring in educational leadership. *International Journal of Qualitative Studies in Education (QSE), 25*(1), 73–87.

CLOSING

Meghan L. Green
Erikson Institute, USA

Relationships over time are at the heart of *Daughters of (Re)Imagined Early Childhood Education: Reflective Narratives of Black Women Educators in Texas During COVID-19*. The stories bestowed in the previous chapters reveal seven Black women early childhood educators' truths about poignant stages in our lives. When I contacted each co-author about participating in this project, I could simply feel that electricity and excitement through the text message thread. I had recently graduated with my doctoral degree and transitioned from the early childhood classroom to higher education as a postdoctoral researcher. My sons, Terry and Camren, and I relocated from Fort Worth, Texas to Chicago, Illinois just two months after the 2021–2022 school year ended. Bobbi, Myah, Krys, Alexis, Carson, and Deidra checked in on us often – sending well wishes and prayers as we attempted to settle into our new space.

We agreed to embark on this journey towards publishing our lived experiences in October 2022. Each step brought another challenge as we navigated personal and professional windfalls. Some of us left the primary campus we initially met at and searched for similar communal spaces in new educational sites. Others transitioned out of the teaching profession altogether, preferring to explore other passion projects as we decided on our next moves. One thing remained constant over the year we worked on this book, however, we found joy in our collective check-ins. When someone was stuck writing or revising their chapter, we would hop on a Zoom call just to see each other's faces and hear familiar voices. This process was new for all of us, but we remained focused on our goal of sharing our stories in the hopes that they would resonate with other educators. Cynthia Dillard

(2019, p. 113) once described the conditions under which Black women scholars feel joy:

- We feel joy when we feel visible and heard.
- We feel joy when we feel respected.
- We feel joy when we feel whole (or, as my mentor/scholar/friend Patti Lather has said, when we feel our fullness).

Her words are encapsulated in our experiences as co-authors, friends, and sisters and are woven throughout the stories we shared in this book. Our joy manifested through connections with our loved ones through a tumultuous ordeal, our faith in things unseen, and our belief in the importance of our voices.

My goal throughout this endeavour persisted. I wanted to open a dialogue about the impact of teaching during dual pandemics. I wanted to emphasize the stories of Black women educators in a way that reverberated with folks who walked through the world unassumingly doing impossible things. These narratives were shared in a spirit of (re)memberance and (re)cognition (Dillard, 2022) of the awe-inspiring ways and being of Black women educators who make syrupy sweet hard iced tea out of lemons. Each chapter in *Daughters of (Re)Imagined Early Childhood Education* extends vulnerability and elucidates the following threads of our narratives as Black women educators: (1) normalization of how we express emotions through transformative growth; (2) utilization of our faith and spirituality as protective factors in everyday life; and (3) celebration of our unapologetic commitment to embodied wellness.

As I sat with our stories, the first collective thread I expounded was the normalization of how we express our emotions through transformative growth as Black women. Storying the lives of Black women demands thoughtful attention to our spoken and unspoken ways of being and knowing (McClish-Boyd & Bhattacharya, 2021, 2023; Turner, 2024). There are lessons in each direct story and lessons peaking just behind the explicit words. In Chapter 1, Bobbi related her process of transformation to a sunflower in her yard that she had come to associate with triumphant feelings. When she had to cut the majestic flower's broken stem to allow it to regrow, she learned that difficult life events sometimes make room for pivoting from one path to another. Myah also considered how her emotional depth acted as a superpower over the years, especially when she has had to process challenging experiences in Chapter 2. Her emotional intelligence, however, was also her lifeline for joyous occasions as she reminded us to give ourselves grace as we strive to find our way.

The second collective thread I identified in our narratives was how we used our faith and spirituality as protective factors in our everyday lives. It is important to note that Black women have defined *faith* and *spirituality* in diverse ways connected to a deeper, more-than-human understanding of the *sacred* (McClish-Boyd & Bhattacharya, 2021; Turner, 2024; Walker, 1983). This deeper understanding may or may not be tied to organized religious affiliations. While Bobbi, Myah, Krys, and Alexis explicitly mention a religious deity in their narratives, Carson, Deidra, and I ruminate on faith through stories about our interpersonal relationships with those around us. In Chapters 3 and 4, Krys and Alexis illuminate how their spirituality guides their lives and how they make sense of the world. In Chapter 7, I describe how my faith is rooted both in my individual practices of self-care and the communal practices surrounding me that centre joy, healing, hope, and care.

As previously mentioned, Black women educators' joy is closely related to feelings of wholeness (Dillard, 2019). For Black women early childhood educators, this sense of wholeness is heavily impacted by our desire to serve and nurture the young children and families in our communities (Edwards et al., 2021). Service without proper attention to one's individual wellness, however, creates a disjointed existence. The final theme I recognized across the stories in *Daughters of (Re)Imagined Early Childhood Education* was each chapter author's unapologetic commitment to embodied wellness. In Chapter 5, Carson noted how her transition from teaching to clinical psychology taught her a valuable lesson on how we see ourselves in relation to others around us. She stated that educators must centre children's humanity before they can effectively engage with them. Deidra's story amplified this concept even further in chapter 6 by revealing the importance of affirming Black women educators' humanity as well. Racialized and gendered systems of oppression have historically and contemporarily placed enormous burdens on Black women to care for everyone but us (Sykes, 2022). Through concerted, intentional efforts, Bobbi, Myah, Krys, Alexis, Carson, Deidra, and I, discovered how to curate the healing spaces we needed to achieve wholeness.

Black women educators' views of Black and Brown children are often grounded in our shared cultural identities and supported by our desires to create and sustain humanizing educational settings (Gardner et al., 2020; Green, 2023; Wynter-Hoyte et al., 2021). Homes are often described as places where hearts, minds, and spirits meet to take time to care for the body. The body may be nourished through physical means, but the other aspects of one's being derive strength from the spirituality that Dillard (2022) described as the unification of Black women's politics, spiritual consciousness, and creativity. This book was our home, our safe haven to transparently story our experiences. Our stories do not subscribe to a White dominant tendency towards linear resolves; our stories pose fluid points of tension and intricacy towards a more nuanced understanding of Black women's lives. I leave readers with a final offering as a means of (re)claiming my responsibility as a Black woman educator and researcher (see Dillard, 2016). A poem that speaks to the freedom dreams of Bobbi, Myah, Krys, Alexis, and Deidra and to the dreams of our ancestors.

'Dreams Realized'

I bet our ancestors' wildest dreams
Included moments when they just sat down and
Took time to give thanks for each other.
Took time to give thanks for the strength that they didn't have to
Show just right at that second
Because some other sista was there to give them a chance to

BREATHE.

I bet our ancestors' wildest dreams
Included moments when they just looked at each other and
Just nodded their heads ever so slightly.
Looked at each other and let a slow grin pass
Over their lips without uttering a word
Because that one act of signifying was more than enough for them to

KNOW.

I bet our ancestors' wildest dreams
Included moments when they laughed without hesitation and
Felt joy deep within their spirits.
Felt the warmth of familiar spaces of sisterhood
While whispering their prayers for us in the wind
Because they knew that joy was the key to

LIBERATION!

REFERENCES

Dillard, C. (2016). Turning the ships around: A case study of (re)membering as transnational endarkened feminist inquiry and praxis for Black teachers. *Educational Studies (Ames), 52*(5), 406–423. https://doi.org/10.1080/00131946.2016.1214916

Dillard, C. (2019). To experience joy: Musings on endarkened feminisms, friendship, and scholarship. *International Journal of Qualitative Studies in Education, 32*(2), 112–117. https://doi.org/10.1080/09518398.2018.1533149

Dillard, C. B. (2022). *The spirit of our work: Black women teachers (re)member.* Beacon Press.

Edwards, E. B., Terry, N. P., Bingham, G., & Singer, J. L. (2021). Perceptions of classroom quality and well-being among Black women teachers of young children. *Education Policy Analysis Archives, 29*(56).

Gardner, R. P., Osorio, S. L., Carrillo, S., & Gilmore, R. (2020). (Re)membering in the pedagogical work of black and brown teachers: Reclaiming stories as culturally sustaining practice. *Urban Education, 55*(6), 838–864.

Green, M. L. (2023). Building culturally situated relationships with BIPOC children through a communal ethic of care. *Early Childhood Education Journal9, 52*(5), 935–948.

McClish-Boyd, K., & Bhattacharya, K. (2021). Endarkened narrative inquiry: A methodological framework constructed through improvisations. *International Journal of Qualitative Studies in Education, 34*(6), 534–548.

McClish-Boyd, K., & Bhattacharya, K. (2023). Methodological considerations for endarkened narrative inquiry. *Qualitative Inquiry, 30*(7), 548–594.

Sykes, M. (2022). Wet nurses, nannies, and mammies. In M. Sykes & K. Ostendorf (Eds.), *Child care justice: Transforming the system of care for young children* (pp. 9–19). Teachers College Press.

Turner, C. R. (2024). Endarkened feminist narrative. In *Encyclopedia of social Justice in education*. Bloomsbury Publishing.

Walker, A. (1983). *In search of our mothers' gardens: Womanist prose*. Harcourt Brace Jovanovich.

Wynter-Hoyte, K., Thornton, N. A., Smith, M., & Jones, K. (2021). A revolutionary love story in teacher education and early childhood education. *Theory Into Practice, 60*(3), 265–278.